W9-CDJ-548

Usama bin Laden's
al-Qaida:
Profile of a
Terrorist Network

Yonah Alexander and Michael S. Swetnam

Transnational Publishers, Inc.

Published and distributed by Transnational Publishers, Inc.
410 Saw Mill River Road
Ardsley, NY 10502, USA

Phone: 914-693-5100
Fax: 914-693-4430
E-mail: info@transnationalpubs.com
Web: www.transnationalpubs.com

ISBN 1-57105-219-4

Copyright (c) 2001 by Transnational Publishers, Inc.

All rights reserved. This book may not be reproduced, in whole or in part, in any form (beyond that copying permitted by U.S. Copyright Law in Section 107, "fair use" in teaching and research, Section 108, certain library copying, and except in published media by reviewers in limited excerpts), without written permission from the publisher.

Manufactured in the United States of America

Table of Contents

About the Authors

Yonah Alexander

A former director of the Terrorism Studies Program at The George Washington University, Prof. Alexander is currently Director, Inter-University Center for Terrorism Studies (affiliated with academic institutions around the world). In addition, he is a Senior Fellow and Director, International Center for Terrorism Studies, Potomac Institute for Policy Studies.

Educated at Columbia University, the University of Chicago, and the University of Toronto, Professor Alexander taught at The George Washington University; The American University; Columbus School of Law at Catholic University of America; Tel Aviv University; the City University of New York; and the State University of New York.

His research experience includes such appointments as Research Professor of International Affairs, The George Washington University; Senior Fellow, the Institute for Advanced Studies in Justice, School of Law, The American University; Senior Staff Member, Center for Strategic and International Studies, Georgetown University; Director, Institute for Studies in International Terrorism, State University of New York; and Fellow, Institute for Social Behavior Pathology, the University of Chicago.

Dr. Alexander is Founder and Editor-in-Chief of the *International Journal on Minorities and Group Rights*. He also founded and edited *Terrorism: An International Journal and Political Communication and Persuasion: An International Journal*. He has published over seventy books on the subjects of international affairs, terrorism, and psychological warfare.

Michael S. Swetnam

Mr. Swetnam founded the Potomac Institute for Policy Studies in 1994 and serves as its President and Chairman. He is currently a member of the technical Advisory Group to the United States Senate Special Select Committee on Intelligence. In this capacity Mr. Swetnam provides expert advice to the U.S. Senate on Research and Development investment strategy of the U.S. intelligence community. Mr. Swetnam also served as a Special Consultant to President George Bush's Foreign Intelligence Advisory Board (PFIAB) from 1990 to 1992 where he provided expert advice on intelligence community issues including budget, community architecture, and major programs. He also assisted in authoring the Board's assessment of intelligence community support to Desert Shield/Storm.

Mr. Swetnam worked for the Director of Central Intelligence (DCI) as a Program Monitor on the Intelligence Community Staff (1986-1990). He was responsible for the development and presentation to Congress of the budget of the National Security Agency and helped develop, monitor, and present to Congress the Department of Energy Intelligence Budget. He was also assigned as the Intelligence Community Staff representative to intergovernmental groups that developed the INF and START treaties. He assisted in presenting these treaties to Congress for ratification. Collateral duties included serving as the host to the DCI's Nuclear Intelligence Panel and Co-Chairman of the Science and Technology Requirements Analysis Working Group.

He has published with Yonah Alexander a four-volume set on *Cyber Terrorism and Information Warfare* (1999).

Preface

Terrorism—the calculated employment of violence, or the threat of violence by individuals, subnational groups, and state actors to attain political, social, and economic objectives in violation of law, intended to create an overwhelming fear in a target group larger than the victims attacked or threatened—is as old as civilization itself. Yet unlike their historical counterparts, present-day terrorists have introduced into contemporary life a new scale of violence in terms of conventional and unconventional threats and impact. The internationalization and brutalization of modern terrorism make it clear that we have entered into an Age of Super and Cyber Terrorism with its serious implications concerning national, regional, and global security concerns. Perhaps the most significant dangers are those relating to the safety, welfare, and rights of ordinary people; the stability of the state system; the health of economic development; the expansion of democracy; and perhaps even the survival of civilization itself.

The academic community—in recognition of its intellectual obligation as well as its moral and practical responsibility to participate in the international effort to arrest the virus of terrorism—has developed in the past four decades multidisciplinary research initiatives focusing on a broad range of issues related to this challenge. For instance, in the aftermath of the February 26, 1993, bombing of the World Trade Center in New York City, the most spectacular foreign terrorist attack in the United States, killing six people and injuring over 1,000 others, the Terrorism Studies Program at The George Washington University organized a research project on the selected Middle East perpetrators. This study grew out of the realization that "if contemporary society is to make terrorism, initiated in the name of supposedly 'higher' ideological and political purposes, a less inviting tactical and strategic tool and a more costly weapon to its precipitators and their nation-state supporters, then it is critical to expand our knowledge of the motivations and capabilities of these groups."[1]

---

[1] Yonah Alexander, *Middle East Terrorism: Selected Group Profiles* (Washington, D.C.: JINSA, 1994), pp.vi-vii.

Americans, and the international community in general, have renewed their interest in the terrorism phenomenon with the emergence of Usama bin Laden's *al-Qaida*. This group has been blamed for: the November 13, 1995, car bomb explosion outside the American-operated Saudi National Guard training center in Riyadh, Saudi Arabia, killing five Americans and two Indians; the June 25, 1996, car bombing attack at Khobar Towers, a U.S. Air Force housing complex in Dhahran, Saudi Arabia, killing 19 soldiers and wounding hundreds more; and the two August 7, 1998 truck bombings outside the U.S. embassies in Nairobi, Kenya and Dar es Salaam, Tanzania, killing 234 people, 12 of them American, and wounding over 5,000 others. *Al-Qaida* is also suspected of mounting the October 12, 2000, suicide bombing of the USS *Cole*, killing 17 and wounding 39 American sailors in Aden harbor, Yemen. Currently, attention has been focused on the unfolding trial at the Southern District Court of New York of four alleged *al-Qaida* members.

It is against this backdrop that the Inter-University Center for Terrorism Studies (a consortia of academic institutions in over 30 countries), in collaboration with the International Center for Terrorism Studies at the Potomac Institute for Policy Studies, initiated a research project to increase our understanding of *al-Qaida*, one of the most notorious contemporary informal and loose international terrorist networks active in some 55 nations. The purpose of this publication is not to glorify bin Laden nor his group. Rather, it is designed to provide an easily accessible reference for academics, policy makers, the press, and other interested individuals. The study exposes much of *al-Qaida*'s mystique and thereby place it in perspective as one of the many challenges facing the international community in the twenty-first century.

We wish to acknowledge the Smith Richardson Foundation, and the Stella and Charles Guttman Foundation for their support of our academic research on this important field of public concern. Neither of the aforementioned foundations bears any responsibility for information contained in this publication.

Important contributions were made by a research team, coordinated by James T. Kirkhope of the International Center for Terrorism Studies, and comprised of: Adam Barrer (Tufts University), Allyson Kozal (Georgetown University), Alon Lanir (Johns Hopkins University), Peter H. Leddy (Tulane University), Brian J. Miller (Georgetown University), Vivek C. Narayanan (American

University), Yoav Rogovin (University of Minnesota), and Mark E. Williams (American University).

In addition to these researchers, other individuals in the United States and abroad have contributed to this project. We are particularly indebted to Professor Herbert M. Levine and Dr. Milton Hoenig of the Inter-University Center for Terrorism Studies and Professor Edgar H. Brenner of the Inter-University Center for Legal Studies (International Law Institute in Washington, D.C) for their review of the manuscript.

Finally, this volume, which represents the first research effort in the Terrorism Library Series of Transnational Publishers, draws on unclassified information generated over the past several years from dozens of international seminars and conferences, numerous interviews, media reports, court cases and field work in the Middle East, Asia, and Europe.

Prof. Yonah Alexander
Senior Fellow and Director
International Center for Terrorism Studies
Potomac Institute for Policy Studies

Mr. Michael S. Swetnam
President and Chairman of the Board
Potomac Institute for Policy Studies

February 28, 2001

Usama bin Laden's *al-Qaida*:
A Profile of a Terrorist Network

al-Qaida (Also Known As)

- al-Qaida, al Qaeda [2]
- al-Qadr [3]
- The International Islamic Front for Jihad Against Jews and Crusaders [4]
- Islamic Salvation Foundation
- The Group for the Preservation of the Holy Sites
- Islamic Army for the Liberation of Holy Shrines [5]
- The Islamic Army for the Liberation of the Holy Places [6]

Brief History

Al-Qaida emerged from the *mekhtab al khidemat* (MAK), the Afghan mujahadeen "services office," around 1989. It serves as an international terrorist network heavily funded and led by its "prince," Usama bin Laden. This loosely knit network is comprised of various terrorist organizations, such as the Egyptian *al-Jihad* and dozens of others. *Al-Qaida* serves as an informal organizational structure for extremist Arab-Afghans, along with thousands of new recruits and supporters in some 55 countries. They are now spreading their *Jihad* (holy war) to all corners of the globe. The *al-Qaida* network has been linked to various terrorist operations, such as the 1993 World Trade Center bombing in New York, the 1996 bombing of the Khobar Towers in Saudi Arabia, the 1998 U.S. embassy bombings in East Africa, and is apparently linked to the attack of the destroyer USS *Cole* in Aden, Yemen, in 2000.

[2] "The Base."
[3] "Night of Power."
[4] U.S. Department of State, *Fact Sheet: Usama bin Laden,* released by the Coordinator for Counterterrorism, August 21, 1998; and *United States v. Usama bin Laden et al.,* S (7) 98 Cr. 1023 (LBS), p. 34. Indictment available at http://www.fbi.gov/majcases/eastafrica/summary.htm.
[5] Refers to the Holy Shrines in Mecca and Medina in Saudi Arabia.
[6] U.S. Department of State, *Foreign Terrorist Organizations Designations 1999,* October 8, 1999, available at www.state.gov/www/global/terrorism/annual_reports.html and *USA v. bin Laden, op. cit.,* pp. 36 and 45.

Ideology and Objectives

- *Al-Qaida* opposes all nations and institutions that are not governed in a manner consistent with the group's particular extremist interpretation of Islam, such as Saudi Arabia.[7]

- *Al-Qaida* opposes the continued presence of the American military in the Middle East, especially on the Arabian Peninsula following the Gulf War.[8]

- In August 1996, Usama bin Laden, *al-Qaida*'s founder, issued a Declaration of Jihad against the United States and the Saudi government.[9]

- In February 1998, Usama bin Laden along with his senior associate Ayaman al-Zawahiri endorsed a fatwah (religious ruling) stating that Muslims should kill Americans, including civilians, anywhere in the world where they can be found. The fatwah was later published in the newspaper *Al-Quds Al-Arabi* on February 23, 1998.[10]

- In May 1998, Mohammed Atef (bin Laden's second in command) sent Khaled al Fawwaz (*al-Qaida*'s spokesman) a letter endorsing a fatwah issued by bin Laden and including a declaration by the "Ulema Union of Afghanistan" calling for a Jihad against the United States and its allies.[11]

- In late May 1998, bin Laden issued a statement entitled "The Nuclear Bomb of Islam," in which he stated that it is the duty of Muslims to prepare as much force as possible to attack the enemies of God.[12]

- A stated objective of *al-Qaida* is to "unite all Muslims and establish a government which follows the rule of the Caliphs." To achieve this goal, all Muslim governments, viewed as corrupted by Western influence, must be overthrown by force. Eventually, Muslim state boundaries will be erased and replaced with a unified government under the rule of the Caliphs.[13]

---

[7] *USA v. bin Laden, op. cit.*, p. 4.
[8] *Ibid.*
[9] U.S. Department of State, *Fact Sheet: The Charges Against International Terrorist Usama bin Laden*, available at www.usembassy.state.gov/posts/af1/wwwh0001.html.
[10] *Ibid.*
[11] *Ibid.*
[12] *Ibid.*
[13] *Ibid.*

Organizational Structure

Al-Qaida has a command and control structure, which includes a *majlis al shura* (or consultation council). The council considers, discusses, and approves major policies and actions, including terrorist operations and the issuing of *fatwahs*. The group has a "military committee" that considers and approves military matters.[14] It also has a business committee, that oversees the *al-Qaida* front businesses and financial matters, a *fatwah* or religious committee, that deliberates religious rulings, a media committee that works on printing information, and a travel office.[15]

LEADERSHIP[16]

Usama bin Laden[17]

aka "Usama bin Muhammad bin Laden"
aka "Usama bin Muhammad bin-'Awad bin Laden"
aka "Shaykh Usama bin Laden"
aka "Abu Abdullah"
aka "Mujahid Shaykh"
aka "Hajj"
aka "Abdul Hay"
aka "al Qaqa"
aka "the Director"
aka "the Supervisor"
aka "the Emir"
aka "the Prince"
aka "the Contractor"

FBI

Usama bin Laden was born in 1957 in Saudi Arabia. He was the seventeenth son of 51 children of Muhammad bin Laden. His father was of Yemeni descent from the village of Al-Ribat; his mother was a Saudi. Muhammad left Al-Ribat in 1931 and founded the Bin Laden Group, a construction company, with his brothers. The company became heavily involved in Saudi government contracts. The group built everything from holy mosques in Mecca and Medina to highways and palaces. From the company the bin Laden family amassed a fortune estimated at billions of dollars.[18]

---

[14] *Ibid*, p. 7.
[15] Statements made by prosecution witness Jamal al-Fadl under oath in Southern District Court of New York February 6, 2001.
[16] *USA v. bin Laden, op. cit.*
[17] "Hunting bin Laden: Who is bin Laden?" PBS Frontline (1999), and *USA v. bin Laden, op. cit.*
[18] John Burns, "Where bin Laden Has Roots, His Mystique Grows." *New York Times*, December 31, 2000.

From an early age, Usama bin Laden was raised as a strict Islamist. Due to his ties with Mecca's mosques and the royal family, his father welcomed many pilgrims during the Hajj season. Others visited even after his father died when bin Laden was thirteen.

It is reported that Usama bin Laden received a civil engineering or public management degree around 1980 from King Abdul-Aziz University in Jeddah, Saudi Arabia. He had two very distinguished teachers: Abdullah Azzam, who later collaborated with him in Afghanistan; and Mohammed Quttub, a famous Islamic philosopher. While Bin Laden was attending the university, the Soviets invaded Afghanistan.

During the early stages of the mujahadeen (Holy Warrior) resistance, bin Laden traveled to Afghanistan and Pakistan to meet with scholars and leaders who had been guests at his family's house. He began lobbying for the mujahadeen and raised large amounts of money for their cause.

After graduation from the university, bin Laden left Saudi Arabia for Afghanistan to join the mujahadeen. Not only did he bring with him fresh recruits, but he also brought construction machinery and large amounts of cash. In 1984, he built a "guesthouse" in Peshawar, Pakistan, which would be the first station for new recruits. From this guesthouse the MAK was born. The MAK, established by Abdullah Azzam, would operate from that location and was active in funneling money into the resistance; building tunnels and hospitals; generating media and publications; and drawing support for the mujahadeen around the world, especially in Afghanistan, but also in places like Yemen. The MAK was known to have a recruiting office in Brooklyn, New York, at the Alkifah Refugee Center.

Around 1986, Usama decided to chart a separate course from MAK. He built his own camps and trained his own fighters. Within two years he had six camps (one he called *al-Masadah*—The Lion's Den). Under his command he ran several successful battles, with help from ex-military advisers from Egypt and Syria who brought much needed experience. He participated in several battles, including the battles of Jalalabaad.

Around 1988, bin Laden realized that it was necessary to keep a documentation of the people who traveled through his "guesthouse," his camps, and Afghanistan. He wanted to be able to track friends and fellow mujahadeen fighters as well as to be able to give answers to families with missing loved ones and friends who were out of touch. This network became known as "*al-Qaida*" (or "the base"). After the Soviet withdrawal from Afghanistan in 1989, he went back to Saudi Arabia. From about 1989 to 1991 *al-Qaida* was headquartered in Peshawar, Pakistan.[19]

The Afghan war, however, did not end with the Soviet departure. The rebels' hostilities continued initially against the Moscow-backed government and then between opposing factions (the Taliban and the Ahmed Shah Massoud group). A car bomb killed Azzam and his two sons in Peshawar, Pakistan, on November 24, 1989, and MAK suffered a major blow.

[19] *USA v. bin Laden, op. cit.*, p. 4.

During the same period in Saudi Arabia, bin Laden gave many public speeches about the Afghan victory, the failures of the Saudi government, and an impending Iraqi invasion. The Saudi government became concerned by his activities and placed a travel ban on him.

After the Iraqi invasion of Kuwait, bin Laden was distraught that the Saudi government had sought and received western governments' help. Consequently, bin Laden met with several religious leaders and began to round up recruits. The Saudi government then attempted to stop his activities.

As a result, bin Laden used his connections to leave the country for Pakistan. After a very short period in Pakistan, he went back into Afghanistan. There he tried to work out a settlement between the warring factions battling for power, while gathering support for a new Jihad. In late 1991, after his efforts at mediation in the Afghani civil war had failed, and several reported attempts were made on his life, bin Laden left for the Sudan.

Bin Laden was attracted to the Sudan for several reasons. First, the strict Islamist ideology of the new regime under the National Islamic Front appealed to him, and the regime sought his help. Also, there was an opportunity for a plethora of construction projects, including major highways, ports, and airports. Bin Laden set up several new companies in the Sudan, which would take on these projects, but would also be used to provide income to support *al-Qaida*'s activities and serve as a front to transport weapons and men. He also found employment and homes for several hundred "Arab-Afghans" who could not or would not return home after the Jihad in Afghanistan.[20]

In the Sudan, bin Laden set up *al-Qaida*'s headquarters in the Riyadh section of Khartoum. It is reported that bin Laden funded and had remote, if not direct, involvement in several terrorist operations in Yemen, Saudi Arabia, Somalia, and Egypt, as well as the World Trade Center bombing in New York, among other bombing incidents. At various times while in the Sudan, bin Laden and other members worked to put aside their differences with the Shiite Muslim organizations and tried to unify them under *al-Qaida* against their common enemies. Bin Laden and *al-Qaida* had talks with some elements within the Government of Iran and the terrorist organization, Hezbollah. It is believed that bin Laden sent members of his group to Hezbollah camps in Lebanon to receive training.[21]

It is reported that while living in the Sudan, Saudi intelligence botched several attempts on his life. The Saudi government froze his assets sometime around 1993 and publicly withdrew his Saudi citizenship in 1994. Usama was also denounced by members of his family. After his public denunciation, bin Laden formed the Advice and Reform Council (ARC) as a political arm. Through the ARC, bin Laden and his associates published several statements condemning the Saudi and western governments. By 1996, the

[20] *Ibid.*, p. 14.
[21] *Ibid.*, p. 15.

Sudan was under extreme international pressure for hosting bin Laden and his followers. The Sudanese government, desiring to lift the embargo against the country, asked bin Laden to leave. He then relocated to Afghanistan.

Since his return to Afghanistan, he has issued several public statements, including a Declaration of Jihad[22] against the United States and several fatwas calling for all Muslims "to kill Americans and their allies, civilian and military, [as] an individual duty."[23] He has set up several training camps for his new Jihad against the United States. From these camps, bin Laden has financed several terrorist operations, such as the Khobar Towers bombing in 1996 in Saudi Arabia and the 1998 bombings of the American embassies in East Africa. Many plots devised by bin Laden have been thwarted by various security agencies around the globe; however, bin Laden's vast network of resources and devoted following enabled him to continue his Jihad. The umbrella framework—the International Islamic Front for Jihad Against Jews and Crusaders—which bin Laden and associates set up in Afghanistan in February 1998 serves as a "clearing house" and coordinating body for many groups worldwide.

He has also survived several attempts on his life [24] including a number of bomb attacks. During the past several years, more than 100 *al-Qaida* members have been arrested in some twenty countries. Bin Laden, however, still enjoys a safe haven in Afghanistan despite the latest sanctions imposed by the United Nations Security Council on December 19, 2000.

Abdullah Ahmed Abdullah

FBI

aka "Abu Mohammed el Masry"
aka "Saleh"
aka "Abu Marium"
aka "Abu Mohammed el Masri Saad al Sharif"

An Egyptian national, but possibly of Saudi origin, and one of five indicted by a U.S. federal grand jury on December 20, 2000, for the 1998 African embassy bombings. Abdullah Ahmed Abdullah faces the death penalty for playing a direct role. He is currently at large.[25] He reportedly played an active role in both embassy bombings as well as the murders of the U.S. servicemen in Mogadishu. During

[22] U.S. Department of State, *Fact Sheet: The Charges Against, op. cit.*
[23] "Fatwa," February 23, 1998, in al-Quds al-Arabi (London), www.ict.org/articles/fatwahh.htm
[24] "Hunting bin Laden" PBS Frontline, *op. cit.*
[25] Dan Eggen and David Vise, "More Indicted in Embassy Attacks," *The Washington Post*, December 21, 2000, p. A15.

the Afghan war he trained soldiers in the use of explosives at the Jihad Wal camp in Khost. It is believed he sat on *al-Qaida*'s consultation council as well as the religious/fatwa committee.[26]

Saif al Adel

aka "Saif"

FBI

Adel, an Egyptian national, was indicted on December 20, 2000, by a federal grand jury. Although it is believed he did not play an active role in the actual bombing of the embassies, it is reported that he sat on *al-Qaida*'s consultation council as well as the military committee. It is also believed he played an active role in Somalia where 18 U.S. servicemen were murdered by *al-Qaida* trained men. He is currently at large.

Muhammed Atef

aka "Abdul Aziz Abu Sitta"
aka "Abu Hafs Taysir"
aka "Abu Hafs el Masry"
aka "Abu Hafs el Masry el Khabir"
aka "Sheik Taysir Abdullah"
aka "Abu Fatima"
aka "Taysir"
aka "Abu Khadija"
aka "Abu Hafs"

FBI

Egyptian national and cofounder of *al-Qaida*. Atef is a member of the majlis al shura and military committee and is the alleged second in command.[27] He is presently at large, indicted for alleged connection in the East African embassy bombings.[28] Atef's daughter is married to bin Laden's son. It is believed that in the event of bin Laden's capture or death, Atef will become *al-Qaida*'s leader.

---

[26] Jamal al-Fadl Statement, *op. cit.*
[27] Jamal al-Fadl Statement, *op. cit.*
[28] FBI Most Wanted.

Abu Ubaidah al Banshiri
(DECEASED)

aka "Aadil Habib"
aka "Galal Fouad Elmelify Abdeldaim"
aka "Jalal"
aka "Adeel Habib"

Cofounder of *al-Qaida* and reported deceased. Banshiri was a member of both the majlis al shura and the "emir" (or head) of the military committee.[29] According to testimony by his brother-in-law, Ashif Mohamed Juma, al-Banshiri drowned in a ferry accident on Lake Victoria in May 1996.[30] The name "Banshiri" derives from the Banshir Valley where he supposedly went when he first arrived in Afghanistan to fight the Soviets. It is believed he was a police officer in Egypt before he went to fight the Jihad in Afghanistan.[31]

Anas al Liby

aka "Anas al Sebai"
aka "Nazih al Raghie"

FBI

A Libyan national who allegedly sat on *al-Qaida's* consultation council. He was indicted in the United States on December 20, 2000, on charges of conspiracy to commit murder, kill U.S. citizens, commit terrorist acts, and destroy U.S. defense installations. He allegedly took photographs of the embassy in Kenya that were later used by bin Laden to pinpoint where the explosives should go.[32]

Omar Mahmoud Othman Omar

aka "Abu Qutadah"
aka "Omar Abu Omar"

Omar, of Palestinian origin and a Jordanian national, obtained political asylum in Britain after being convicted twice *in absentia* by a Jordanian court for his connections to terrorist activities. Jordanian officials have asked for his extradition, due to his previous involvement in planned attacks and to his involvement in *al-Qaida*. He was arrest

[29] *USA v. bin Laden, op. cit.,* p. 7.
[30] Statements made by prosecution witness Ashif Mohamed Juma under oath in the Southern District Court of New York on February 14, 2001.
[31] Jamal al-Fadl Statement, *op. cit.*
[32] "Five More People Indicted," CNN, *op. cit.,* and Jamal al-Fadl Statement, *op. cit.*

ed by British authorities in early February 2001, but was released without charge.[33] However, British officials have stated that he is required to return to the police station for further questioning on February 26. He has known ties with the Armed Islamic Group (GIA) and is a known fundraiser for the Chechen rebels.[34] Omar has been pointed out by Jamal al-Fadhl in his testimony in the Southern District Court of New York on February 6, 2001, as a member of *al-Qaida*'s Fatwa Committee under the name "Abu Qutadah."[35]

Mamdouh Mahmud Salim

aka "Abu Hajer"
aka "Abu Hajer al Iraqi"

FBI

An Iraqi, Salim was born in 1958 and established links between *al-Qaida* and groups in Iraq and Lebanon. He was arrested in Germany on September 16, 1998, and is currently in custody at the Metropolitan Correctional Center in Manhattan. It is believed that Salim cofounded *al-Qaida*. It is reported that Salim managed some camps and guesthouses in Afghanistan and Pakistan, as well as extensive financial dealings within *al-Qaida* and bin Laden's front companies.[36] On November 20, 2000, Salim stabbed a prison guard in the eye, stabbed another in the body, and sprayed irritants on others during a failed escape.[37] He now faces a separate trial from that of the four others currently on trial because of this incident.[38]

[33] Laura King, "Bin Laden Links Sought Amid Arrests," Associated Press, February 21, 2001.
[34] Judith Miller and Sarah Lyall, "Hunting bin Laden's Allies, U.S. Extends Net to Europe," *New York Times*, February 21, 2001.
[35] Jamal al-Fadl Statement, *op. cit.*
[36] *USA v. bin Laden, op. cit.*, pp. 11 and 12.
[37] Larry Neumeister, "5 More Indicted in Embassy Bombings," Associated Press, December 21, 2000.
[38] Joe Lauria, A Wide Plot to Kill Americans Alleged in Embassy Bomb Trial, *Boston Globe*, February 6, 2001, National/Foreign, p. A11

Ayman al-Zawahiri

aka "Dr. Ayman al-Zawahiri"
aka "Abu Muhammad"
aka "Abu Muhammad Nur al-Deen"
aka "Muhammad Ibrahim"
aka "Abu Abdullah"
aka "Abu al-Mu'iz"
aka "The Doctor"
aka "The Teacher"
aka "Ustaz"
aka "Abdel Muaz"
aka "Nur"

FBI

An Egpytian co-founder of *al-Qaida* and member of the group's *shura* council as well as the religious/fatwa committee.[39] He is a leading Islamic militant and is dedicated to the overthrow of Mubarak's government in Egypt for the establishment of an Islamic state. He is the leader of the Egyptian Islamic Jihad, and the relatively new faction called Talaa'al al-Fateh (Vanguards of Conquest). The group was responsible for the assassination of Egyptian President Anwar Sadat and the attempted assassination of President Hosni Mubarak in Ethiopia. He is currently at large.[40]

MEMBERS

Members of *al-Qaida*, whose numbers are unknown, pledge an oath of allegiance called *bayat*. Regular internal investigations of members and associates help the network to detect informants. *Al-Qaida* kills those suspected of collaborating with enemies. A special effort is made by the movement to recruit Americans, as people with U.S. passports can travel freely without raising suspicion. It has been estimated that as many as 5,000 militants have been trained in a dozen camps operated by *al-Qaida* in Afghanistan.[41] These members are the active terrorists who carry out the mission of the organization.

Ahmed Abdullah

A Yemeni arrested in Pakistan with two suspected members of Harakat ul-Mujahedeen on April 2, 2000.[42]

[39] Jamal al-Fadl Statement, *op. cit.*
[40] FBI Most Wanted, *op. cit.*
[41] Stephen Engelberg, "One Man and a Global Web of Violence," *New York Times*, January 14, 2001, pp. 1 and 12-13; and *USA v. bin Laden, op. cit.*, pp. 4 and 11-12.
[42] "An Arrest in Embassy Bombings," *New York Times*, April 3, 2000, p. A8; and *USA v. bin Laden, op. cit.*, pp. 4 and 11-12.

Mustafa Mahmoud Said Ahmed

An Egyptian charged with the bombing of the U.S. Embassy by the Tanzanian Magistrates Court on September 21, 1999. The Egyptian Government has also charged him with terrorist activities in that country. Raised in Zaire, he attended Al Azhar University in Cairo, Egypt, receiving a degree in agricultural engineering. He claims to have worked for the Kuwaiti Defense Ministry until the Iraqi invasion in 1990. He then returned to Zaire and worked with Mobutu Sese Seko. In 1994, he relocated to Tanzania, along with Wadih el Hage (a former personal secretary of bin Laden), and set up a gem business.

Nabil Abu Aukel

A Palestinian who established *al-Qaida*'s first cell in the Palestinian Authority. He underwent advanced training in explosives in bin Laden's Abu Khabab camp in Afghanistan in 1998. Nabel cooperated closely with the Palestinian group Hamas and was arrested by Israel in June 2000.[43]

Ahmed Mohammed Hamed Ali

aka "Ahmed the Egyptian"
aka "Shuaib"
aka "Abu Islam al Surir"

FBI

Ali, an Egyptian national, is one of five indicted by a U.S. federal grand jury on December 20, 2000, for the 1998 East African embassy bombings. Faces up to life in prison for his involvement. He is currently at large.[44] He reportedly did not play a direct role in the 1998 embassy bombings, but he did help train the Somalian gunmen who murdered 18 U.S. servicemen in 1993. American authorities are currently holding a man named Ihab Ali who may or may not have a relation to this man.

Mushin Musa Matwalli Atwah

aka "Abdel Rahman al Muhajer"
aka "Abdel Rahman"

FBI

Indicted December 20, 2000 for involvement in the 1998 embassy bombings. He is charged with conspiracy to commit murder, kill U.S. citizens, commit terrorist acts, and destroy U.S. defense installations. It is reported that he trained *al-Qaida* followers in camps in the Sudan, Pakistan, and Afghanistan. Atwah is presently at large.[45]

---

[43] Judith Miller, "Killing for the Glory of God, In a Land Far From Home," *New York Times*, January 16, 2001, p. A9.
[44] Eggen and Vise, "More Indicted," *op. cit.*
[45] "Five More People Indicted," CNN, *op. cit.*

Adel Mohammed Abdul Almagid Abdul Bary

aka "Adel Abdel Bary"
aka "Abbas"
aka "Abu Dia"

Egyptian
State
Information
Service

An Egyptian born June 24, 1960.[46] Bary managed guesthouses and training camps for *al-Qaida*. It is believed that he was appointed to head the London cell of the Egyptian Islamic Jihad in 1996.[47] Bary was also a member of the Advice and Reform Council. Arrested in London along with Ibrahim Eidarious in July 1999, he is currently fighting extradition to the United States where he faces the death penalty. It is reported that his fingerprints, as well as Eidarious', are on a fax of a 1998 bin Laden fatwah and on other London office documents taking responsibility for the embassy bombings. Bary has been previously convicted and sentenced to death *in absentia* by an Egyptian court for terrorist acts, such as the attempted bombing of the Khan al Khaili, a tourist landmark in Cairo.[48] He is also wanted by Egyptian authorities for his involvement in the al-Gama'a al-Islamiyya organization.[49]

Ibrahim Hussein Abdelhadi Eidarous

aka "Ibrahim Eidarous"
aka "Daoud"
aka "Abu Abdullah"
aka "Ibrahim"

Eidarous, an Egyptian national, was arrested along with Adel Bary in London in July 1999. He is accused of running a London cell for *al-Qaida*, mostly used as a publications and travel office. He reportedly kept contact with *al-Qaida*'s top command through a network of satellite phones. American officials claim Eidarous' fingerprints, along with Bary's, were on a fax of bin Laden's February 1998 fatwa. They also believe his fingerprints to be on faxes claiming responsibility for the embassy bombings which were sent to various media outlets around the world. He also provided fake documentation to several members traveling through Europe and the Middle East. It is believed that Eidarous was previously a member of the Egyptian Islamic Jihad before it merged with *al-Qaida*.

---

[46] Egyptian State Information Service, "Wanted: A Call to Combat Terrorism."
[47] *Ibid.*, p. 25.
[48] Simon Apiku, "Wanted: Terrorists Living Abroad," *Middle East Times*, January 27, 1999.
[49] Egyptian State Information Service, "Wanted" *op. cit.*

Mustafa Mohamed Fadhil

aka "Moustafa Ali Elbishy"
aka "Mustafa Fazul"
aka "Hussein"
aka "Hassan Ali"
aka "Abu Jihad"
aka "Khalid"

FBI

Fadhil has both Kenyan and Egyptian citizenship. He was indicted in the Southern District of New York, on December 16, 1998, for his alleged involvement in the August 7, 1998, bombings of the U.S. embassies in Dar es Salaam, Tanzania and Nairobi, Kenya, and for conspiring to kill U.S. nationals. Fadhil is presently at large.[50] He faces the death penalty if captured for playing a direct role in the embassy bombings.

Jamal Ahmed al-Fadl

Fadl, born in the Sudan, was the first witness for the prosecution in the embassy bombings trial in New York City. According to his own sworn testimony, he left *al-Qaida* in 1996, after he stole approximately $110,000. He supposedly made plans with Saudi intelligence to assassinate bin Laden after fleeing the group, but instead turned to the U.S. government offering information for protection. He was recruited to fight in Afghanistan by Mustafa Shalabi at the Al Farooq Mosque in Brooklyn. At the end of the war, he swore allegiance to *al-Qaida*. There, he transported weapons and other members through bin Laden's front companies. While on the stand he identified Wadih el-Hage as a member of *al-Qaida*. In addition, Fadl spoke of the group's efforts to acquire uranium and bin Laden's contacts within Hizballah and Sudanese intelligence.[51]

Khalid Al Fawwaz

aka "Khaled Abdul Rahman Hamad al Fawwaz"
aka "Abu Omar"
aka "Hamad"
aka "Khaled Fawwaz"

Fawwaz reportedly set up a media information office in London and headed the "Advice and Reform Committee." The London office was designed to publicize the statements of bin Laden as well as to provide a cover activity in support of *al-Qaida*'s "military" activities, including recruitment, the disbursement of

[50] FBI Most Wanted, *op. cit.*
[51] Colum Lynch, "Witness Tells How Bin Laden Group Works," *Washington Post*, February 7, 2001.

funds, the procurement of funds, and procurement of equipment. The London office also served as information center which collected reports from various *al-Qaida* cells, including the Kenyan cell, and translated them to headquarters. It is also believed that Fawwaz helped to establish businesses in Kenya as fronts, particularly Asma Limited. He then supposedly transferred ownership to Banshiri in 1994.[52] He was arrested on September 28, 1998 in London and is fighting extradition to the United States where he could face life in prison.

Ahmed Khalfan Ghailani

aka "Ahmed the Tanzanian"
aka "Abu Khabar"
aka "Abu Bakr"
aka "Foopie"
aka "Abubakary Khalfan Ahmed Ghailani"
aka "Shariff Omar Mohammed"

FBI

Ahmed Ghailani is a Tanzanian national. He was indicted in the Southern District of New York, on December 16, 1998, for his alleged involvement in the August 7, 1998, bombings of the U.S. embassies in Dar es Salaam, Tanzania and Nairobi, Kenya. He is presently at large.[53] Ghailani could face the death penalty if captured and convicted for his direct involvement in the embassy bombings.

Wadih el Hage

aka "Abdus Sabbur"
aka "Abd al Subbur"
aka "Norman"
aka "Wa'da Norman"
aka "Wadia"
aka "Abu Abdullah al Lubnani"
aka "the Manager"

FBI

Born in Sidon, Lebanon, on July 25, 1960, he attended the University of Southwestern Louisiana where he received a bachelors degree in urban planning. El Hage has been indicted on multiple counts of perjury pertaining to his relationship with *al-Qaida*.[54] In 1993, el Hage was in Sudan where he met with bin Laden and became his personal sec-

[52] *USA v. bin Laden, op. cit.*, pp. 8 and 18; and Phil Hirschkorn and Deborah Feyerick, "Embassy Bombings Trial Witness says Bin Laden Wanted to Buy Uranium," CNN, February 7, 2001.
[53] FBI Most Wanted, *op. cit.*
[54] Tom Hays, "Embassy Bombing Defendants," Associated Press, February 4, 2001.

retary. In 1994, he relocated to Nairobi and registered with the Kenyan government as a representative of Africa Help, a humanitarian organization supposedly based in Heidelberg, Germany. German authorities have no record of such an organization. He also set up several businesses used as covers, including Tanzanite King. El Hage listed Aadil Habib as one of the organization's local officers. Habib was also known as Abu Ubaidah al Banshiri, cofounder and top military commander of *al-Qaida*, who died in a boating accident on Lake Victoria in 1996. [55] El Hage worked for a variety of bin Laden's front companies.[56] El Hage left Nairobi shortly after being questioned by the FBI.[57] He was arrested on September 20, 1998, and has been in custody since. He contends that he was never part of any terrorist organization and that he worked solely for bin Laden's legitimate businesses and this is a possibility.

Zein-al-Abideen Mohammed Hussein

aka "Abu Zubayday"

A 27-year-old Palestinian veteran of the Afghan war and coordinator for external operations of *al-Qaida*. Responsible for communications between bin Laden and operative cells worldwide, Abu Zubaydah assigns members screened at his Peshawar, Pakistan, guesthouse to *al-Qaida* training camps in Afghanistan. His whereabouts are unknown.[58]

L'Houssaine Kherchtou

Kherchtou, a 36-year old Moroccan, testified in the embassy bombings trial on February 21, 22, 26, and 27, 2001 as a government witness. In his sworn testimony he told the court he had joined *al-Qaida* in 1991 and worked for the group in Kenya. He fingered el-Hage as the person who oversaw the operation in Kenya in 1994 and 1995. Kherchtou also identified el-Hage as a member of *al-Qaida*. He also pointed Odeh as another *al-Qaida* member who went to Somalia in 1993.[59] During cross-examination by attorneys for el-Hage, Kherchtou contradicted himself, stating that he was not sure that el-Hage was a member of *al-Qaida*.[60]

---

[55] *USA v. bin Laden, op. cit.*, p. 18.
[56] *USA v. bin Laden, op. cit.*, p. 14.
[57] "Hunting bin Laden," PBS Frontline, *op. cit.*
[58] Miller, "Dissecting a Terror Plot," *op. cit.*, pp. A1 and A7.
[59] Phil Hirschkorn, "Bin Laden the Focus of Embassy Bombing Trial," CNN, February 21, 2001.
[60] Phil Hirschkorn, "Witness Backtracks at Embassy Bombings Trial," CNN, February 27, 2001.

Ali Abdelseoud Mohamed

aka "Abu Omar"
aka "Omar"
aka "Ahmed Bahaa Eldin Mohamed Adam"[61]
aka "Taymour Ali Nasser"

US
Army
Tape

Born in Egypt, Ali Mohammed is a naturalized American citizen. He is the only known person to plead guilty to the charges in the embassy bombings indictment. He spent several years in both the Egyptian and American military, using these skills to train jihad warriors in Afghanistan, the Sudan, and the United States. He is suspected of facilitating bin Laden's 1991 relocation from Peshawar, Pakistan, to Sudan. It is also believed that Mohamed traveled to Canada in order to smuggle other members of *al-Qaida* into the United States.[62] It is also believed Mohamed provided communications equipment and security training to the *al-Qaida* bodyguard unit and members of the Sudanese intelligence service who were protecting bin Laden in the Sudan.[63] He was taken into U.S. custody on September 10, 1998.

Fazul Abdullah Mohammed

aka "Abdallah Fazul"
aka "Fazul Abdilahi Mohamed"
aka "Fazul Abdallah"
aka "Fazul Mohammed"
aka "Harun"
aka "Harun Fazul"
aka "Fazhl Khan"

FBI

Fazul Mohammed has duel citizenship in the Comoros Islands and Kenya. He was indicted on September 17, 1998, in the Southern District Court of New York, for his alleged involvement in the bombings of the U.S. embassies in Dar es Salaam, Tanzania, and Nairobi, Kenya, on August 7, 1998.[64] A senior aid to Wadih el Hage, he prepared reports for bin Laden and his top lieutenants. Fazil lived with el Hage in Nairobi until moving into his own residence a few weeks before the bombing. It was in this new residence that the bomb was partly assembled. Charged with 12 counts of murder, murder conspiracy, and the use of weapons of mass destruction. His whereabouts are unknown. He was last reported seen in the Comoro Islands.

---

[61] *USA v. bin Laden, op. cit.*, p. 18.
[62] *Ibid.*, p. 20.
[63] *Ibid.*, pp. 13, 14, 16, and 22.
[64] FBI Most Wanted, *op. cit.*

Khalfan Khamis Mohamed

aka "Zahran Nassor Maulid"

FBI

Khalfan Khamis Mohamed, a Tanzanian
national, was indicted on December 16, 1998,
in the Southern District Court of New York, for
his alleged participation in the August 7, 1998,
bombings of the U.S. embassies in Dar es Salaam, Tanzania and Nairobi, Kenya, and
for conspiring to kill U.S. nationals. He allegedly received training in Afghanistan.[65] It
is believed that Mohamed assembled the Tanzanian bomb and flew to South Africa
shortly after the bombing. On October 5, 1999, he was arrested in Cape Town, South
Africa.[66] On November 2, 2000, Mohamed and Mamdouh Mahmud Salim (another
al-Qaida member) attacked a federal prison guard in a failed escape attempt, critically
injuring him.[67] In February 2001, his trial began in New York.[68]

Fahid Mohammed Ally Msalam

aka "Fahad M. Ally"

A Kenyan national, was indicted on December
16, 1998, in the Southern District Court of
New York, for his alleged involvement in the
August 7, 1998, bombings of the U.S.
embassies in Dar es Salaam, Tanzania and
Nairobi, Kenya, and for conspiring to kill U.S.
nationals. He is currently at large.[69]

FBI

Abdallah Nacha

A Lebanese national who supposedly filmed the U.S. embassy in Nairobi four days
before the bomb exploded. Nacha was quickly apprehended soon after the blast. It is
reported that he, along with others, ran a fish business funded by bin Laden in Nairobi
as a front for the *al-Qaida* operation.[70]

---

[65] *USA v. bin Laden, op. cit.*, p. 22.
[66] Benjamin Weiser, "Man Charged in Bombing of U.S. Embassy in Africa," *New York Times*, October 9,
1999, p. A4; and FBI Most Wanted, *op. cit.*
[67] Jim Dwyer and Greg B. Smith, "Two Plotted Prison Attack for Days," *New York Daily News*, November
3, 2000, p. 8.
[68] Tom Hays, "Embassy Bombing Defendants," *op. cit.*
[69] FBI Most Wanted, *op. cit.*
[70] Stephen Muiruri, "Three Suspects Picked for Filming Embassy," *Daily Nation* (Nairobi), August 22, 1998.

Mohammed Saddiq Odeh

aka "Abu Moath"
aka "Noureldine"
aka "Marwan"
aka "Hydar"
aka "Abdullbast Awadah"
aka "Abdulbasit Awadh Mbarak Assayid"

FBI

A Jordanian national who joined *al-Qaida* in 1992, Odeh received training in various camps in Afghanistan. In 1993, he relocated to Somalia to train Islamic troops opposed to U.S. involvement. In 1994, Odeh moved to Mombasa, Kenya, and established a fishing business using *al-Qaida* funds to be used as a cover. On several occasions he was visited by top aides, including Atef and Banshiri.[71] Odeh was arrested in Karachi, Pakistan, on August 7, 1998, the day of the embassy bombings. He was detained after his flight from Nairobi. He was then extradited to Kenya on August 16, 1998, and subsequently handed over to the United States, where he was charged on August 28, 1998, in connection with the Nairobi Embassy bombing.[72] On February 28, 2001, FBI Special Agent John Anticev testified that Odeh told him that the Nairobi bombing was a "blunder" since many Kenyan civilians were killed in the attack.[73] Anticev also testified that Odeh believed members of *al-Qaida*, especially Abdullah Ahmed Abdullah, were responsible for the bombing, although Odeh specifically denied any involvement in the bombing.[74]

Mohamed Rashed Daoud Owhali

aka "Khalid Salim Saleh bin Rashed
aka "Moath"
aka "Abdul Jabbar Ali Abdel-Latif"

FBI

Taken into U.S. custody and charged on August 27, 1998, with conspiracy to commit murder, use of a weapon of mass destruction, and 12 counts of murder. He reportedly got out of the Nairobi bomb truck just before detonation and threw a stun grenade at the security guard in front of the U.S. embassy.[75] He suffered injuries to his back, hands, and face as a result of the Nairobi embassy bombing. He has met with bin Laden on several occasions.

[71] *USA v. bin Laden, op. cit.*, pp. 14 and 17.
[72] Tom Hays, "Embassy Bombing Defendants," *op. cit.*
[73] Statement made by prosecution witness FBI Special Agent John Anticev in the Southern District Court of New York on February 28, 2001; Phil Hirschkorn, "Agent: Defendant called Kenya Attack a 'Blunder'," CNN, February 28,2001; and Gail Appleson, "Bin Laden Follower Says Colleagues Did Bombing," Reuters, February 28, 2001.
[74] John Anticev, Statement, *op. cit.*
[75] *USA v. bin Laden, op. cit.*, p. 44; "Confession Allowed in Terrorist Case," *San Diego Union-Tribune* (Reuters), January 30, 2001, News, p. A-5; and Greg B. Smith, "Trial Begins in Bombing of Embassies, " *Daily News*, February 6, 2001, News, p. 24.

Abdurrahman Husain Mohammed Al-Saafani

aka "Mohammed Omar al-Harazi"
aka "Abdul Rahman Hussein Al-Nashari"
aka "Abdul Rahman Hussein Al-Nassir"

Established the first *al-Qaida* cell in Saudi Arabia. Attempted to smuggle antitank missiles and was arrested in 1997. He reportedly was involved in the failed attack on the U.S. warship USS *The Sullivans* in Aden in January 2000. Subsequently, he fled to Kandahar, Afghanistan, where he was based at an *al-Qaida* guesthouse.[76] He is also the prime suspect in the USS *Cole* bombing. Saafani has been identified by Yemeni authorities as the man who was the operations leader of the *Cole* attack.[77] It is reported that his cousin was the suicide bomber in the Nairobi attack, named in the indictment as "Azzam".[78]

Sheikh Ahmed Salim Swedan

aka "Sheikh Bahamadi"
aka "Ahmed Ally Bahamad"
aka "Ahmed the Tall"

FBI

A Kenyan national, he was indicted on December 16, 1998, in the Southern District of New York, for his alleged involvement in the August 7, 1998, bombings of the U.S. embassies in Dar es Salaam, Tanzania and Nairobi, Kenya, and for conspiring to kill U.S. nationals. He is presently at large.[79]

---

[76] Miller, "Killing for the Glory of God," *op. cit.*
[77] "US, Yemen Closing in on Top USS *Cole* Suspect—Paper," Reuters; February 10, 2001.
[78] "USS *Cole* Plot Began After Embassy Attacks, Investigator Says: Suicide Bomber Identified," CNN, December 20, 2000.
[79] FBI Most Wanted, *op. cit.*

ASSOCIATES

The associates to *al-Qaida* may not have pledged the "bayat" to the group or bin Laden, but are equally important. These men assist *al-Qaida* by providing intelligence, money, and equipment, as well as recruitment. They might also be part of a separate organization or cell, yet receive support, funding, and/or training through the *al-Qaida* network. It is possible some associates would collaborate with *al-Qaida* on several occasions, but still maintain autonomy from the inner group.

Hamid Aich

An Algerian suspected of involvement in plot to smuggle explosives into the United States from Canada. After moving to Burnaby, British Columbia, he lived with Abdel Majid Dahoumane (a member of the Armed Islamic Group). Moved to Ireland in May 1999 where Irish authorities arrested him, seized his computer, and searched his apartment in December of that year. Aich was released before authorities discovered material linking him to the bomb plot.[80]

Maulana Masood Azhar

Since his release from an Indian prison in 1999, Azhar has lead the Jaish Mohammed, a splinter group from the Harakat ul-Mujahideen.[81] His group is supposedly closely linked with the Taliban and bin Laden. Many of his fighters have been trained in Afghanistan camps or have taken part in the war there.

Abdel Salem Boulanouar

A French-Algerian with ties to Ahmed Ressam, Fateh Kamel, and the Moro Islamic Liberation Front. Arrested June 24, 2000, in Paris after being deported from the Philippines.[82]

Bouabide Chamchi

An Algerian national and suspected member of the Algerian Armed Islamic Group. Chamchi was arrested while entering the United States with an illegal passport on December 19, 1999, at the Beecher Falls, Vermont/Canadian border.[83]

[80] David Johnston, "Evidence Is Seen Linking bin Laden to Algerian Group," *New York Times*, January 27, 2000, p. A1.
[81] Zahid Hussain, "Dozen Rebel Groups Wage Unrelenting War Against India," *The Times* (UK), December 28, 2000.
[82] Donald G. McNeil Jr., "French Hold Suspected Terrorist Tied to bin Laden," *New York Times*, June 28, 2000, p. A4.
[83] David A. Vise and Lorraine Adams, "Bin Laden Weakened, Officials Say," *Washington Post*, March 11, 2000, p. A3.

Abdelmajid Dahoumane

U.S. Department
of State

Dahoumane, an Algerian, is a believed accomplice of Ahmed Ressam with links to the GIA. He shared a room with Ressam in Vancouver shortly before Ressam was arrested at the Canadian-American border in Port Angeles, Washington, on December 14, 2000. Dahoumane was then indicted by a federal grand jury for his involvement in the bomb plot but eluded authorities until December 2000 when he was reportedly arrested in Algeria.[84]

Khalil Sa'id Deek

aka "Khalil Al-Deek"
aka "Abu Eiyad"
aka "Khalil Alvi"

A naturalized American of Palestinian descent. Arrested in Peshawar, Pakistan, and extradited to Jordan on December 17, 1999. Deek is charged with conspiring to bomb the American-owned Radisson Hotel in Amman. Deek was arrested in Peshawar, Pakistan, while holding a disk containing the "Jihad Encyclopedia." It contains information on bomb construction. He is believed to arrange travel for *al-Qaida* operatives.[85]

Maulana Ghafoor Haideri

Central Secretary General of the Jamiat Ulema-e-Islam group, which has close ties with *al-Qaida*. Haideri has stated publicly that if Afghanistan or bin Laden were to be attacked, his group would retaliate against Americans.[86]

Mustafa Ahmed Hassan Hamza

aka "Abu Hazem"
aka "Mohamed Gamal El-Sayed"
aka "Mohamed Gamal El-Sayed Ali Khalil"

Egyptian State
Information Service

Hamza, an Egyptian national, born December 14, 1957. He is reported to be the commander of the military branch of the Islamic Group. He was sentenced to death *in absentia* by an Egyptian court in the Returnees from Afghanistan case. It is believed he took part in the 1981 assassination of Egyptian President Anwar Sadat, the attempted assassination

---

[84] Andrea Koppel and David Ensor, "Suspect in Alleged U.S. Millennium Plot Arrested in Algeria." CNN, December 7, 2000.
[85] Jack Kelley, "Terrorists Use Web to Mount Attacks," *Arizona Republic*, February 6, 2001, p. A9.
[86] "JUI Warns Washington," *Gulf News* (Dubai), October 31, 2000.

of President Mubarak in 1995, and the Luxor massacre, as well as an attempted assassination of Egyptian Interior Minister Zaki Badr.[87] Hamza was in Khartoum with bin Laden in the early 1990s when he ordered the Luxor attack and helped coordinate Mubarak's assassination. Bin Laden helped to finance and cover for many of Hamza's activities. There are reports that Hamza lives in London, Peshawar, and Afghanistan.[88]

Sheik Mir Hamzah

He has previously been arrested by Indian authorities in 1993, but was subsequently released. Emir of the Jaimat-ul-Ulema-e-Pakistan and cosigner of the February 23, 1998, fatwa published in the *Al Quds Al Arabi* newspaper.

Mokhtar Haouari

An Algerian national, based in Montreal, suspected of planning the logistics for the attempted bombing by Ahmed Ressam. He has been accused of forging documents and papers to facilitate travel of *al-Qaida* members. He is a suspected member of the Algerian Armed Islamic Group and was arrested in Montreal, January 10, 2000.[89]

Raed Mohamed Hassan Hijazi

aka "Abu Ahmed the American"
aka "Abu Ahmed the Mortarman"
aka "Raed Hejazi"

An American citizen born in 1969 in California, Hijazi graduated from California State University in Sacramento. He grew up in Jordan and Saudi Arabia and converted to Islam. From early 1997 to late 1998 he lived in Boston and was a taxi driver. He supposedly contributed some $13,000 of his savings from driving a taxi to the Jordan millennium bomb plot. Trained in 1999 in Afghanistan in explosives and mortars, Hijazi traveled extensively in many countries including Pakistan, Israel, Turkey, and the United Kingdom. He was involved in recruiting new members for *al-Qaida* and purchased materials such as sulfuric and nitric acid for explosives to be used in the Jordan plot. Hijazi was linked to Abu Hoshar in the conspiracy and was sentenced to death *in absentia* by a Jordanian military court in September 2000.[90] Later that month, he was arrested by Syrian authorities in Damascus and extradited to Jordan where he has since been cooperating with the authorities.[91]

---

[87] Egyptian State Information Service, "Wanted," *op. cit.*
[88] Simon Apiku, "Wanted," *op. cit.*; "Luqsor Massacre: Shedding the Light on the Western Support for Terrorism," *Al Sha'ab Al-Arabi*, translated by HIPRS, January 1, 1998; and "Egypt Says bin Laden Paid Luxor Gunmen," Reuters, May 13, 1999.
[89] Vise and Adams, "Bin Laden Weakened," *op. cit.*, and Larry Neumeister, "Millennium Bomb Plotter Cops Plea," Associated Press, March 9, 2001.
[90] James Risen, "Foiled Terror Plot on Tourists Linked to bin Laden Aide," *New York Times*, February 29, 2000, p. A1; and Judith Miller, "Dissecting a Terror Plot from Boston to Amman," *New York Times*, January 15, 2001, pp. A1 and A7.
[91] "Syria Said to Deport Convicted Muslim Militant," *Gulf News* (Dubai), December 4, 2000.

Khader Abu Hosher

The ringleader of the Jordan plot, he was arrested on November 30, 1999 with 15 co-conspirators and is now awaiting execution in Jouweideh prison, Jordan. Born some 36 years ago in Jordan to a Palestinian refugee family. He participated in the war against the Soviets in Afghanistan. Hoshar then joined a radical group in Jordan seeking to overthrow King Hussein by force. He was arrested, sentenced to death, and then pardoned. In 1993, he moved to Yemen where he established a link with the Palestinian Islamic Jihad. Hoshar then returned to Jordan where he was arrested and imprisoned for 18 months. He was released in 1998 and arranged for four Jordan operatives to be trained in advanced explosives in Afghanistan. He himself was trained there in the late 1980s, stayed at the guesthouse of Abdullah Azzam in Pakistan, and linked with Abu Zubayday, *al-Qaida*'s coordinator for "external operations."[92]

Mohamed Ahmed Shawqi el-Islambouli

aka "Abu Khaled Nasser"
aka "Abu Ja'far"
aka "Shawqi Shaheen Mohammed el-Kurdi"
aka "Abdel-Fattah Abdel Hameed Abu-Zaid"
aka "Khalid Waleed Abdul Wadoud"
aka "Mahmoud Youssef"

Egyptian State
Information Service

Mohamed Islambouli, born in 1955, is the brother of Khaled Islambouli, Egyptian President Anwar Sadat's assassin. He was sentenced to death *in absentia* by an Egyptian in court in the "Returnees from Afghanistan" case.[93] A top official in Gama's Islamyia (Islamic Group), Islambouli is reported to be living in Afghanistan.[94]

Eyad Ismoil

Coconspirator in the World Trade Center bombing, Ismoil was arrested in Jordan in 1995. After extradition to the United States, he was convicted November 13, 1997 of conspiracy and sentenced to 240 years in prison, fined $250,000, and ordered to pay $10 million in restitution.

---

[92] *Ibid.*
[93] Egyptian State Information Service, "Wanted," *op. cit.*
[94] "Egypt Sentences 9 to Death in Biggest Trial Militants Ever," CNN, April 18, 1999; and "Luqsor Massacre," *Al Sha'ab Al-Arabi*, *op. cit.*

Osama Rushdy Ali Khalifa

aka "Abu-Mos'ab al-Seidi"
aka "Ali Mohammed Abu Kamel"

Born in 1959 and associated with Sheik Omar Abdel-Rahman, Kalifa is considered a coordinator for Egypt's Islamic Group at home and abroad.[95]

Egyptian State
Information Service

Fateh Kamel

Former owner of the Artisanat Nord-Sud craft store in Montreal that was subsequently transferred to Mokhtar Haouari.   He was arrested by Jordanian authorities on December 15, 1999, and extradited to France to stand trial for an alleged subway bomb plot. French authorities believe he is a leader of the Groupe Roubaix, a group of Islamic bombers and robbers who fund Islamic causes through criminal acts. His trial in Paris began February 7, 2001 along with 23 others. Seven are being tried *in absentia*, including Ahmed Ressam, who is in U.S. custody. Over the course of the trial he admitted to his connections with Ressam in Canada, but denied any criminal activity.[96]

Youssef Karroum

A Moroccan national arrested January 28, 2000, when trace explosives were found on his car. He is listed by the U.S. Department of State as a known associate of Ahmed Ressam and is being held as a material witness in Ressam's case.

Saeed Awad Al-Khamri

(DECEASED)

aka "Abdullan Ahmed Khaled Al-Mousawa"

Al-Khamri was one of the two suicide bombers in the attack of the USS *Cole* in October 2000. Al-Khamri was from the Yemeni province of Hadhramaut, where bin Laden's family also originates.[97] Al-Khamri, using the "Al-Mousawa" alias, rented the boat used on the *Cole* attack and also leased a house overlooking the Aden harbor to observe any American ships for possible attacks.[98]

---

[95] Egyptian State Information Service, "Wanted," *op. cit.*, and Simon Apiku, "Wanted," *op. cit.*
[96] Elaine Ganley, "Islamic Militants Trial Begins," Associated Press; February 7, 2001, and Verena Von Derschau, "Defendant: Apartment Was for Meetings," Associated Press, February 16, 2001.
[97] David Ensor, Chris Plante, and Peter Bergen, "USS *Cole* Plot Began After Embassy Attacks, Investigator Says," CNN, December 20, 2000.
[98] *Ibid.*

Mustafa Labsi

An Algerian national with links to the Groupe Roubaix, he reportedly rented the apartment where Ahmed Ressam stayed in Canada. He was arrested in London by British authorities in early February 2001 and was charged with possessing computers, electronics, false identification papers, and credit cards, along with large sums of money "which give rise to reasonable suspicion" that he was planning along with others a terrorist attack.[99]

Abdel Ghani Meskini

Meskini is a Nigerian native and a suspected member of the Armed Islamic Group. He traveled from New York City to Seattle with forged identification to meet Ahmed Ressam. Meskini was arrested December 30, 1999 in Brooklyn[100]after authorities found his information in Ressam's car. He has testified that he conspired with Mokhtar Haouari to provide assistance to Ressam's planned attack. Authorities had intercepted a call from Meskini to an unidentified source in Algeria in December 1999 in which he spoke of Houari's and Ressam's links to a well-organized group. Meskini has pleaded guilty to all counts against him and has decided to cooperate with U.S. authorities. He faces a maximum of 105 years in prison.[101]

Essam Al-Ridi

Al-Ridi, a naturalized American born in Egypt in 1958, testified for the prosecution in the Southern District Court of New York on February 14, 2001. Al-Ridi, a flight instructor, was a veteran of the Afghanistan conflict where he first met bin Laden and el Hage in 1983.[102] During the 1980s, Al-Ridi shipped night vision goggles and rifles to the *mujahadeen.* In 1993, Al-Ridi purchased a used jet for bin Laden with el Hage as the go-between. The jet was to be used to transport Stinger antiaircraft missiles to Khartoum, but the missiles were never shipped. Al-Ridi did shuttle *al-Qaida* members to Nairobi using the plane, at the same time that *al-Qaida* established the Nairobi cell. In 1994, he crashed the plane and fled, ending his association with *al-Qaida.* Al-Ridi testified that he grew disillusioned with bin Laden and *al-Qaida*, stating that he was opposed to a "rich man with no military experience trying to be a decision maker."[103]

---

[99] Judith Miller and Sarah Lyall, "Hunting bin Laden's Allies," *op. cit.*
[100] Vise and Adams, "Bin Laden Weakened," *op. cit.*
[101] Mike Carter, "Feds Link Ressam to Terror Camps," *Seattle Times*, March 9, 2001, and "Nigerian Man Agrees to Cooperate in Millennium Terrorist Plot," CNN, March 8, 2001.
[102] Sworn testimony of Essam Al-Ridi at the Southern District Court of New York, February 14, 2001.
[103] Deborah Feyerick and Phil Hirschkorn, "Witness Says He Bought Plane, Made Shipments for bin Laden," CNN, February 14, 2001.

Maulana Fazlur Rehman

Rehman is a veteran of the Afghan War, a leader of Harkat ul-Mujahideen. and secretary general of the Jamiat Ulema-e-Islam party. He still commands Afghan warriors and is believed to have close financial and military ties with bin Laden and *al-Qaida*.[104] He has stated that if the United States would attack Afghanistan or Usama bin Laden, his group would retaliate against Americans. It is also reported that he has a 313-member armed guard with instructions to kill anybody suspected of harming him.[105] Rehman is also a cosigner of the fatwah published on February 23, 1998, in *Al Quds Al Arabi* as the leader of the Jihad movement in Bangladesh. In the fatwa he states it is every Muslim's duty to kill Americans wherever and whenever possible.

Ahmed Ressam

aka "Abu Reda"
aka "Benni Antoine Noris"

Ressam is an Algerian national and suspected member of the Armed Islamic Group GIA. He was arrested December 14, 1999, at Port Angeles, Washington, while trying to smuggle illegal explosives and timers into the United States from Canada in an attempt to possibly attack during the millenium celebrations. The French government contends he is a member of the Groupe Roubaix, a cell of the GIA which operated in and around the town of Roubaix, France. The cell carried out several violent attacks around the town in the mid-1990s until a shoot-out with an elite French police team left several members dead in 1996. He is currently being tried, along with 23 others, *in absentia* by a French court for his role in this group, which funded Jihad groups in Bosnia and Afghanistan through a series of violent robberies. Many believe Ressam fought in Bosnia against the Serbs and Croats in the early-mid 1990s. French authorities also have Ressam as a possible suspect in the 1996 Port Royal bombing, a rush-hour subway attack in Paris that killed four and injured 91 others. On trial as well is Fateh Kamel, said to have led the Roubaix gang. American authorities believe Ressam was in *al-Qaida* camps during the cruise missile attacks, yet survived. They maintain that he has spent over a year in an Algerian prison for allegedly trafficking weapons to extremist groups in the early 1990s.[106] Ressam has pleaded not guilty to making false statements, transporting explosives, and possessing an illegal firearm among other charges, and his American trial is set to start in Los Angeles on March 12, 2001.

Maulana Salahuddin

Salahuddin is the leader of the Hezb ul-Mujahadeen guerilla group based in Muzaffarbad, Pakistan-controlled Kashmir, a strong ally of the Taliban and bin Laden's cause. He is also the supreme commander of the United Jihad Council, an umbrella organization for 14 Kashmiri militant groups.[107]

---

[104] Zahid Hussain, "Dozen Rebel Groups," *op. cit.*
[105] "JUI Warns Washington," *Gulf News, op.cit.*
[106] Mike Carter, "Feds Link Ressam", *op. cit.*
[107] Zahid Hussain, "Dozen Rebel Groups," *op. cit.*

Hafiz Saeed

Saeed is a former university professor of Islamic studies in Pakistan. He is now the leader of the Lashkar-i-Tayaba, a major guerrilla group in Kashmir.[108]

Khaled Al-Saafani

Khaled Al-Saafani holds both Yemeni and Bosnian passports. He and his family were deported from Kuwait to Bosnia on November 11, 2000. It is reported he was running a "honey business" and had links to *al-Qaida* in Kuwait. Apparently Saafani, along with Youssuri Ahmed and others, planned to carry out a "big operation" inside Kuwait as well as other places for *al-Qaida*. The two men were caught with five hand grenades and 113 kilos of high explosives.[109] It is not known if he is any relation to Abdurrahman Husain Mohammed Al-Saafani.

Osama Sumar

A Palestinian with a forged Saudi passport, Sumar was involved in the abortive 1999 bombing plot in Jordan. He built an underground chamber to store chemical ingredients to be used for explosives. Arrested by the Jordanian authorities, Sumar disclosed the location of a cell safe house.[110]

Refai Ahmed Taha

aka "Refai Ahmed Taha Moussa"
aka "Abu Yasser"
aka "Abdel-Hai Ahmed Abdel Wahab"
aka "Essam Ali Mohammed Abdallah"
aka "Salah Ali Kamel"
aka "Thabet"
aka "Ezz"

Egyptian State
Information Service

Taha, leader of the Egyptian Islamic Group's shura council, was a signatory of *al-Qaida*'s 1998 fatwa under the banner "The Islamic International Front for the Struggle Against Crusaders and Jews." However, it has been reported that Taha has had a falling out with bin Laden and has tried to distance Gama'a Islamyya away from *al-Qaida*.[111] He was sentenced to death in Egypt in the "Returnees from Afghanistan" case.[112] Funded by bin Laden, he has also been linked to the assassination of Anwar Sadat.[113]

---

[109] "Kuwait Deports Egyptian, Bosnian as Suspected Terrorists," *Gulf News* (Dubai), Reuters, November 11, 2000, and "Haled AL Safani, Suspected of Being Connected with bin Laden, Deported to BH," Radio Banja Luka News, Tuzla Night Owl (Brcko), November 12, 2000.
[110] Miller, "Dissecting a Terror Plot," *op. cit.*
[111] Jailan Halawi "Bin Laden Behind Luxor Massacre?" *Al-Ahram Weekly*, May 20-26, 1999.
[112] Egyptian State Information Service, "Wanted," *op. cit.*
[113] *Ibid.*, and Ahmed Ismail, "Senior Islamist Activist May Be Under Arrest," *Middle East Times*, June 16. 2000.

Abdel Hakim Tizgha

An Algerian national and suspected member of Armed Islamic Group. Arrested December 24, 1999, in Bellevue, Washington, shortly after the arrest of Ahmed Ressam.[114] He is a member of the network which includes Ressam, Dahoumane, Houari, and Meskini which tried to attack during millennial celebrations. He pleaded guilty to several conspiracy charges in the fall of 2000.[115]

Hussein Turi

An Algerian national involved in the Jordan plot. Served as a link between Abu Hosher and Abu Zubaydah. Turi carried a forged French passport and had hidden material for the Jordan attack in his home in the Weidhat refugee camp in Amman, Jordan. He is now under arrest in Jordan and cooperates with the authorities.[116]

Ramzi Yousef

Yousef is a veteran of the Afghan War and was trained in explosives. He was the bomb maker for the 1993 World Trade Center attack. Yousef was arrested in Pakistan on February 7, 1995, while staying in a bin Laden "guest house" in Peshawar. He was convicted on November 13, 1997, of conspiracy and sentenced to 240 years in prison.

US Department
of State

Bakht Zamin

Leader of the Al-Badar group, a splinter faction of the Hezb ul-Mujahadeen. Zamin reportedly fought in the Afghan war and his group carries out attacks in Kashmir repeatedly. The group vows to defend bin Laden at any and all cost.[117] A commander of his, Naseer Ahmed Mujahid, reportedly met with bin Laden in 1999.

Muhammad Rabie al-Zawahiri

Brother to Ayman and former member of the Egyptian Jihad's Shura Council. He was arrested in the United Arab Emirates and extradited to Egypt where the FBI questioned him in February 2000.[118]

---

[114] Vise and Adams, "Bin Laden Weakened," *op. cit.*
[115] Mike Carter, "Feds Link Ressam" *op. cit.*
[116] Miller, "Dissecting a Terror Plot," *op. cit.*
[117] Zahid Hussain, "Dozen Rebel Groups," *op. cit.*
[118] Ahmed Ismail, "Senior Islamist," *op. cit.*

Financial Sources of Support

Al-Qaida's activities are largely supported by Usama bin Laden. He has long financed operations with his personal fortune, at one time estimated between $270 to $300 million, from the bin Laden Group, his father's construction company.[119] After settling in the Sudan, bin Laden set up various companies, such as a holding company known as Wadi al Aqiq, a construction business known as Al Hijra, an agricultural company known as al Themar al Mubaraka, an investment company known as Ladin International, an investment company known as Taba Investments, a leather company known as the Khartoum Tannery, and a transportation company known as Qudarat Transport Company.[120] He greatly increased his fortune with these new companies as he was given very high profile construction projects by the Sudanese government. He also nearly monopolized many export industries, such as sesame and corn products. However, *al-Qaida* was able to use these companies to provide cover for the procurement of explosives, weapons, and chemicals, and the transportation of operatives and to make large amounts of money.[121]

Other than bin Laden, *al-Qaida* continues to receive support throughout the world to continue its jihad. The network has reportedly been receiving additional funds from various sources in the Middle East. In 1999, the Saudi Arabian government uncovered a group of Islamic clergy who had been funneling an estimated $50 million in donations given in the form of alms to bin Laden.[122] It is believed that *al-Qaida* has also received funds through the Dubai Islamic Bank in Dubai, which is controlled by the United Arab Emirates.[123] The Saudi Arabian government has detained Khalid bin Mahfouz, a wealthy Saudi banker, for laundering contributions from Saudi businessmen through his bank.[124] The United States has traced several companies and charitable aid organizations that are suspected of raising and laundering funds for *al-Qaida*. One of these charitable organizations is the Mercy International Relief Agency.[125]

Some of *al-Qaida's* operations are financed through personal savings of operatives, robberies, and commercial activities by individuals and businesses.

---

[119] Scott Macleod, "The Paladin of Jihad," *Time Magazine* 147, no. 19 (May 6, 1996).
[120] *USA v. bin Laden, op. cit.*, pp. 13-14.
[121] *Ibid.*
[122] "Bin Laden Said to Get Millions from Wealthy in Gulf," *Boston Globe*, July 7, 1999, p. A10.
[123] James Risen and Benjamin Weiser, "U.S. Officials Say Aid for Terrorists Came Through Two Persian Gulf Nations," *New York Times*, July 8, 1999, p. A1.
[124] Jack Kelley, "Saudi Money Aiding bin Laden: Businessmen Are Financing Front Groups," *USA Today*, October 29, 1999, p. 1A.
[125] *Ibid.*

Groups Affiliated with *al-Qaida*[126]

The Advice and Reform Committee[127]
Asbat al Ansar (Lebanon)
Harakat ul-Ansar/Mujahadeen (Pakistan)
Al-Badar (Pakistan)
Armed Islamic Group/GIA (Algeria)
Saafi Group for Proselytism and Combat (GSPD) (Algeria)
Talaa al Fath (Vanguards of Conquest)
The Groupe Roubaix (Canada/France)
Harakat ul Jihad (Pakistan)
Jaish Mohammed (Pakistan)
Jamiat-ul-Ulema-e-Pakistan (Pakistan)
Jamiat Ulema-e-Islam (JUI/Pakistan)
Hezbollah (Lebanon)
Hezb ul-Mujahideen (Pakistan)
al-Gama'a al-Islamiyya (Islamic Group, Egypt)
al-Hadith (Pakistan)
Hamas (Palestinian Authority)
Bayt al-Imam (Jordan)
Islamic Jihad (Palestinian Authority)
Islamic Movement of Uzbekistan
al-Jihad (Bangladesh)
al-Jihad (Egypt)
al-Jihad Group (Yemen)
Laskar e-Toiba (Pakistan)
Lebanese Partisans League
Libyan Islamic Group
Moro Islamic Liberation Front (Philippines)
Partisans Movement (Kashmir)
Abu Sayyff (Philippines)
Al-Ittihad (Somalia)
Ulema Union of Afghanistan[128]

---

[126] Michael Sheridan, "Hostages Trapped," *op. cit.*; U.S. Department of State, *Patterns of Global Terrorism*, 1999, *op. cit.*; and *USA v. bin Laden*, *op. ci*t., pp. 6, 7, and 15
[127] "Hunting bin Laden," PBS Frontline, *op. cit.*
[128] *USA v. bin Laden*, *op. cit.*, p. 34.

Areas of Operation[129]

Al-Qaida, being a truly international network with links in some 55 countries, is not limited to a specific area of operations. It has vowed to strike against its adversaries around the world.[130] The following is a partial list of the areas of the network's operations:

MIDDLE EAST

Egypt, Iraq, Iran, Israel, Jordan, Kuwait, Lebanon, Libya, Morocco, Palestinian Authority Areas, Saudi Arabia, Sudan, Syria, Tunisia, Turkey, United Arab Emirates, and Yemen.

ASIA

Afghanistan, Bangladesh, China, India (Kashmir), Indonesia, Malaysia, Myanmar, Pakistan, and the Philippines.

EUROPE

Albania, Belgium, Bosnia, Croatia, Denmark, France, Germany, Italy, Kosovo, Luxembourg, the Netherlands, Spain, Sweden, Switzerland, and the United Kingdom.

FORMER SOVIET UNION

Azerbaijan, Russia, Chechnya, Tajikistan, and Uzbekistan.

AFRICA

Algeria, Comoros Islands, Djibouti, Eritrea, Ethiopia, Kenya, Libya, Mauritania, Nigeria, Senegal, Somalia, South Africa, Sudan, Tanzania, Uganda, and Zaire.

NORTH AMERICA AND SOUTH AMERICA

Canada, United States, Argentina, Brazil, Paraguay, and Uruguay[131]

---

[129] *USA v. bin Laden, op. cit.*, pp. 7-8, and 107; U.S. Department of State, *Fact Sheet: Usama bin Ladin, op. cit.*
[130] U.S. Department of State, *Fact Sheet: Usama bin Ladin, op. cit.*
[131] "Uruguayans Arrest bin Laden Associate," Prepared by the B'nai B'rith Center for Public Policy, February 1999.

Headquarters

Al-Qaida's previous base of operations was near the city of Peshawar, Pakistan. In or about 1991 *al-Qaida* and its leadership relocated to the Sudan, remaining there until 1996 and then moved to Afghanistan.[132]   In May 1999, it moved to Farmihadda, Afghanistan, a few miles south of Jalalabaad near the Pakistani border. The operation took a home in an ex-military base known as Tora Bora. This site was a key base of the Hezb-i-Islami faction of Younus Khales during the Soviet occupation. It is now under Taliban control.[133] *Al-Qaida*'s headquarters has subsequently moved with Usama bin Laden throughout a number of camps in eastern Afghanistan, including the Zhawar Kili camps. These particular camps, along with the El Shifa chemical factory in Khartoum, came under fire from American tomahawk missiles in 1998 .

U.S. Department of Defense

Tactics and Capabilities

Al-Qaida's tactics include bombing, hijacking, kidnapping, assassination, and suicide attacks. Reportedly, the group is actively seeking weapons of mass destruction (nuclear, chemical, and biological weapons).[134] *Al-Qaida* has been linked to the production of the chemical VX in Sudan and the production of the biological agent ricin. On several occasions the group has tried to obtain enriched uranium.

[132] *USA v. bin Laden, op. cit.*, p. 4.
[133] "Osama Moves to Tora Bora base in Afghanistan." *Business Recorder* (Pakistan), March 18, 1999.
[134] Central Intelligence Agency, Statement by Director of Central Intelligence George J. Tenet before the Senate Select Committee on Intelligence on "The Worldwide Threat in 2000: Global Realities of Our National Security," February 2, 2000, available at www.odci.gov/cia/public_affairs/speeches/dci_ speech _ 020200.html.

Targets and Attacks

December 29, 1992

A bomb explodes in a hotel in Aden, Yemen. The bomb was intended to kill U.S. troops en route to Somalia, but the servicemen had already left the premises. Two Austrian tourists were killed in the blast. It is believed that this was the first attack involving *al-Qaida*.

February 23, 1993

A large bomb exploded in the basement of the World Trade Center killing eight people and injuring more than 1,000. The spiritual leader behind the attack was Sheik Omar Abdel-Rahman. The bomb maker was Ramzi Yousef who stayed in a bin Laden "guest house" in Peshawar, Pakistan, both before and after the bombing. Both men have been arrested, convicted, and are serving multiple life sentences in the United States.

October 3 and 4, 1993

Eighteen U.S. troops are killed in Mogadishu, Somalia, by suspected *al-Qaida*-trained terrorists.

June 26, 1995

Attempted assassination on the life of Egyptian President Hosni Mubarak, in Addis Ababa, Ethiopia.

November 13, 1995

Five Americans and two Indians are killed when a car bomb explodes outside of an American-operated Saudi National Guard training center in Riyadh, Saudi Arabia.

June 25, 1996

A massive truck bomb explodes outside the Khobar Towers, a U.S. Air Force housing complex in Dhahran, Saudi Arabia, killing 19 U.S. servicemen and wounding over 500.

August 7, 1998

On the anniversary of the ordering of U.S. troops into the Gulf region, two large bombs detonate minutes apart outside U.S. embassies in Nairobi, Kenya, and Dar es Salaam, Tanzania. The explosions killed 234, including 12 Americans, and injuring more than 5,000.

October 5, 2000

Suicide bombers attack the USS *Cole*, killing 17 and wounding 39 American sailors in Yemen; *al-Qaida* suspected.

Arrests of a*l-Qaida* Members and Associates

Ahmed Abdullah
Arrested in Pakistan with two suspected members of Harakat ul-Mujahedeen on April 2, 2000.

Mahmud Abouhalima
Convicted March 4, 1994, in the World Trade Center bombing.

Ahmed Mohammad Ajaj
Convicted March 4, 1994, in the World Trade Center bombing.

Nabil Abu Aukel
Arrested by Israel in June 2000.

Nidal Ayyad
Convicted March 4, 1994, in the World Trade Center bombing.

Adel Mohammed Abdul Almagid Abdul Bary
In custody in London, Bary is currently fighting extradition to the United States where he faces the death penalty for his role in bombing the U.S. embassies in East Africa.

Abdel Salem Boulanouar
Arrested June 24, 2000, in Paris after being deported from the Philippines.

Bouabide Chamchi
While entering the United States with an illegal passport, Chamchi was arrested December 19, 1999, at Beecher Falls, Vermont.

Khalil Sa'id Deek
Arrested in Peshawar, Pakistan, and extradited to Jordan on December 17, 1999. Deek is charged with conspiring to bomb the American-owned Radisson Hotel in Amman.

Ibrahim Hussein Abdelhadi Eidarous
Arrested in London and currently fighting extradition to the United States where he could face the death penalty for his role in bombing U.S. embassies in East Africa.

Abdel Ghani
Arrested December 30, 1999, in New York in connection with Ahmed Ressam.

Mokhtar Haouari
Arrested in Montreal, January 10, 2000.[135]

---

[135] Vise and Adams, "Bin Laden Weakened," *op. cit.*

Raed Hijazi
Arrested October 2000 in Syria and extradited to Jordan where he has since been cooperating with the authorities.

Khader Abu Hosher
Arrested on November 30, 1999, in Jordan with another 15 co-conspirators and is now awaiting execution in Jouweideh prison, Jordan.

Eyad Ismoil
Ismoil was arrested in Jordan in 1995. After extradition to the United States, he was convicted November 13, 1997, of conspiracy in the World Trade Center bombing and sentenced to 240 years in prison, fined $250,000, and ordered to pay $10 million in restitution.

Mohammed Kahlid
Accused of participating in the Kenya bombing and is currently in custody.

Fateh Kamel
Arrested by Jordanian authorities on December 15, 1999, he was extradited to France to stand trial for an alleged subway bomb plot.

Youssef Karroum
Arrested January 28, 2000. Associate of Ahmed Ressam and is being held as a material witness.

Abdel Ghani Meskini
He traveled from New York City to Seattle with forged identification to meet Bouabide Chamchi. Arrested December 30, 1999 in Brooklyn.

Ali Mohamed
He was taken into U.S. custody in September 1998. Now Mohamed is a witness for the U.S. government.

Khalfan Khamis Mohamed
On October 5, 1999, he was arrested in Cape Town, South Africa, and is now in a U.S. federal prison.

Mohammed Saddiq Odeh
Arrested in Pakistan on August 7, 1998, the day of the Nairobi embassy bombings. He was detained on a flight from Nairobi to Karachi, Pakistan. He was extradited to the Kenyan authorities on August 16, 1998, and subsequently handed over to the United States, where he was charged on August 28, 1998, in connection with the Nairobi embassy bombing.

Mohamed Rashed Daoud Owhali
Taken into U.S. custody and charged on August 27, 1998, with conspiracy to commit murder, use of a weapon of mass destruction, and murder for the embassy bombing in Kenya.

Sheik Omar Abdel-Rahman
He was arrested and convicted on October 1, 1995, in connection with the plot to blow up the United Nations, Federal Plaza, and the Lincoln and Holland tunnels. Sheik Rahman was also charged with seditious conspiracy. He was sentenced to multiple life sentences.

Ahmed Ressam
Ressam was arrested December 14, 1999, at Port Angeles, Washington, while trying to smuggle illegal explosives and timers into the United States from Canada.

Mohammad Salameh
Convicted March 4, 1994, in the World Trade Center bombing.

Mamdouh Mahmud Salim
He was arrested in Germany in 1998 and currently is in custody at the Metropolitan Correctional Center in Manhattan. On December 20, 2000, Salim stabbed a prison guard in the eye and another in the body, and sprayed irritants on others during a failed escape. He will now face a separate trial from the trial of the four others at the Southern District Court of New York because of this incident.

Osama Sumar
Arrested by the Jordanian authorities, Sumar was involved in the abortive 1999 bombing plot in Jordan.

Jamal Tahrawi
Suspected of being involved in a plot to attack tourist sites in Jordan. Arrested May 23, 2000, in Amman, Jordan.

Hussein Turi
An Algerian national involved in the Jordan plot, he is now under arrest in Jordan and cooperates with the authorities.

Ramzi Yousef
The bomb maker for the 1993 World Trade Center bombing. Yousef was arrested in Pakistan on February 7, 1995, and convicted on November 13, 1997, for conspiracy and sentenced to 240 years in prison.

al-Qaida Timeline[136]

1979-1984

Soviet troops invade Afghanistan. Bin Laden relocates to Afghanistan to help the effort of the mujahadeen.[137]

Along with Abdallah Azzam, a Palestinian scholar and leader of the Palestinian Muslim Brotherhood, bin Laden organizes MAK, a recruiting office to help the Afghan resistance movement. The MAK opens recruiting offices throughout the world, including the United States and Europe. Bin Laden finances the transportation of the new recruits to Afghanistan where they are trained in camps built on land donated by the Afghan government. Bin Laden also uses his personal fortune to employ experts in warfare, sabotage, and covert operations to train the recruits.[138]

1981

President Anwar el-Sadat of Egypt is assassinated by radical Muslims seeking to overthrow the government and replace it with an Islamic state based on "sharia," or Islamic law.

1986

Al Masadah, a training camp for Arab fighters recruited in the Gulf states, is founded by bin Laden. Also, Mustafa Shalabi, an Egyptian immigrant, creates the *Alkifah* Refugee Center in Brooklyn, New York, at the *Al Farooq* Mosque. It later relocates to 566 Atlantic Avenue, where the center serves as a MAK office used to raise money and recruit fighters to help the Afghan mujahadeen.

1988

Bin Laden, Mohammed Atef, and Abu Ubaidah al Banshiri cofound *al-Qaida* to continue the Jihad globally. *Al-Qaida* is headquartered in Afghanistan and Peshawar, Pakistan.

Al-Qaida is instrumental, along with the Egyptian groups *al-Gama'a al-Islamiyya* and *al-Jihad* and the National Islamic Front in Sudan, in the creation of the International Islamic Front for Jihad Against the Jews and Crusaders. The objective of this new organization is to organize Islamic militants throughout the world in order to eradicate non-Islamic governments and replace them with governments based on *sharia*.

---

[136] *USA v. Bin Laden, op. cit.*
[137] Kenneth R. Timmerman, "This Man Wants You Dead," *Reader's Digest Magazine*, July 1998, available at www.readersdigest.com/rdmagazine/specfeat/archives/thismandead.htm.
[138] U.S. Department of State, *Fact Sheet: Usama bin Ladin, op. cit.*

1989

When the Soviet Union withdraws from Afghanistan, bin Laden returns to Saudi Arabia to work in his family's Jeddah-based construction company and to oppose the existing regime and the U.S. intervention in the Middle East.

Egypt's Sheik Omar Abdel-Rahman becomes the spiritual leader of the Arab-Afghans, a group of an estimated 10,000 Afghan war veterans. The Saudi Arabian government holds bin Laden's passport to prevent him from solidifying contacts with Islamic extremists whom he had met during the Afghan war.

1990-1991

Sheik Omar Abdel-Rahman escapes house arrest in Egypt. After fleeing to Sudan, he obtains a visa from the U.S. Embassy sponsored by Mustafa Shalabi, founder of the *Alkifah* Refugee Center in Brooklyn. After a trip to Peshawar, Pakistan, Sheik Rahman arrives in New York.

Rabbi Meir Kahane, leader of the militant Jewish Defense League, is assassinated in New York City by El Sayyid A. Nosair, an Egyptian, one of Sheik Omar Abdel-Rahman's followers.

Wadih el Hage is called by Mustafa Shalabi to come to New York to help resolve a conflict between Shalabi and Sheik Abdel Rahman.

Shortly after el Hage's trip to New York, Shalabi is found murdered in his Brooklyn apartment.

Iraq invades Kuwait, and the United States forms an international coalition and sends troops to Saudi Arabia. Distraught over the American presence near the holy cities of Mecca and Medina, bin Laden decides to move his base elsewhere.

1991-1994

Welcomed by National Islamic Front in Sudan (NIF) Leader Hasan al-Turabi, bin Laden relocates to the Riyadh section of Khartoum, Sudan. Bin Laden begins to increase his personal fortune as well as make contacts with wealthy NIF members by using his construction company, *el-Hijrah* for Construction and Development Ltd., to undertake civil infrastructure development projects. *El-Hijrah* builds the *Tahaddi* road linking Khartoum with Port Sudan and a modern airport near Port Sudan. During this same period, bin Laden's *Wadi al-Aqiq* Company, Ltd., along with his *Taba* Investment Company, Ltd., nearly monopolizes major Sudanese exports of gum, sesame, sunflower, and corn products.

The work force employed by bin Laden's companies grows to mainly consist of veterans from the Afghan war who are unable to return home after the war due to accusations of terrorism and subversive activities. It has been estimated that in May 1993, bin Laden finances the travel of 300 to 480 Afghan war veterans to Sudan.

1992
Civil war in Afghanistan begins. In Algeria, former Arab-Afghani fighters, under the umbrella of the radical fundamentalist movement GIA, launched a campaign of terrorism against the government and secular institutions and persons.

al-Qaida declares that the U.S. military in Saudi Arabia, Yemen, and the Horn of Africa should be attacked.

September 1992
Ramzi Yousef leaves a bin Laden operated "guest house" in Peshawar, Pakistan, and, using a false name, flies to New York.

Ali Mohamed begins training top commanders of *al-Qaida* in Khost, Afghanistan.

December 29, 1992
al-Qaida's first official attack. A bomb explodes in a hotel in Aden, Yemen. The bomb was intended to kill U.S. troops en route to Somalia on a U.N. relief mission, but the troops had already left the premises.

Late 1992-1993
Muhammed Atef travels to Somalia on several occasions for the purpose of determining how to attack U.S. forces.

1993
Ali Mohamed begins training *al-Qaida* operatives in Khartoum, Sudan.

February 23, 1993
A bomb is detonated in the World Trade Center, killing six people and injuring over a thousand. The convicted bomb maker, Ramsi Yousef, had lived in a bin Laden-operated "guest house" in Peshawar, Pakistan, both before and after the bombing.

Spring 1993
al-Qaida sends Ali Mohamed to build training camps in Somalia in order to provide military training and assistance to Somali tribes opposed to UN intervention.

June 25, 1993
Mir Amal Kansi, a Pakistani, opens fire outside of the CIA killing two and wounding three CIA employees. Kansi flees the United States for Pakistan.

October 3-4, 1993
Eighteen U.S. servicemen are killed in Mogadishu, Somalia, by persons trained in *al-Qaida* camps.

1994

Mohamed Sadeek Odeh, an *al-Qaida* operative, relocates to Mombasa, Kenya, and using *al-Qaida* funds, opens a fishing business.

Wadih el Hage, an *al-Qaida* operative, relocates from Khartoum, Sudan to Nairobi, Kenya, and opens multiple businesses using *al-Qaida* funds.

March 1994

Bin Laden's eldest brother, Bakr bin Laden, expresses his family's "regret, denunciation and condemnation" of bin Laden's activities.

April 1994

The Advisory and Reform Committee is created, which produces literature critical of the Saudi Arabian regime and has links to *al-Qaida*.

April 9, 1994

The Saudi Arabian government revokes bin Laden's citizenship for behavior that "contradicts the Kingdom's interests and risks harming its relations with fraternal countries."

1994-1995

al-Qaida camps begin training members of the Algerian Armed Islamic Group. Some of the GIA operatives bomb the Paris Metro, killing eight people.

February 7, 1995

Ramzi Yousef is arrested in Pakistan and extradited to the United States.

June 26, 1995

There is an attempted assassination on the life of Egyptian President Hosni Mubarak in Addis Ababa, Ethiopia.

November 13, 1995

A car bomb explodes outside of an American-operated Saudi National Guard training center in Riyadh, Saudi Arabia, killing five Americans and two Indians. Four Saudi attackers linked to bin Laden were convicted and executed.

Spring 1996

Abu Ubaidah al Banshiri, cofounder and a military leader of *al-Qaida*, drowns when his ferry sinks in Lake Victoria.

1996

Trying to improve relations with the West and have the embargo lifted, the Sudanese government forces bin Laden to leave the country. *Al-Qaida* relocates to Kandahar, Afghanistan, accepting safe haven from the new government of the Taliban.

June 25, 1996
A massive car bomb explodes outside the Khobar Towers, a U.S. Air Force housing complex in Dhahran, Saudi Arabia, killing 19 Americans and wounding hundreds more.

August 23, 1996
From the Hindu Kush Mountains in Afghanistan, bin Laden issues a declaration of Jihad, entitled "Message from Usama Bin-Muhammad Bin-Laden to His Muslim Brothers in the Whole World and Especially the Arabian Peninsula: Declaration of Jihad Against Americans Occupying the Land of the Two Holy Mosques; Expel the Heretics from the Arabian Peninsula."

Afterwards, bin Laden makes an audio tape recording of the declaration for worldwide distribution.

March 19, 1997
A bomb explodes in Jalalabaad, Afghanistan, inside a police station, killing more than 50 people. The bomb is believed to have been an attempted assassination of Usama bin Laden.

November 1997
Four American oil workers are gunned down in Pakistan.

November 13, 1997
Ramzi Yousef and Eyad Ismoil are convicted of conspiracy in the 1993 World Trade Center bombing. Each is sentenced to 240 years in prison.

February 23, 1998
Bin Laden, along with *al-Gama'a al-Islamiyya*, al Jihad, the Jihad movement in Bangladesh, and the Pakistan Scholars Society, endorses a *fatwah* under the guise of the "International Islamic Front for Jihad on the Jews and Crusaders."

The *fatwah* states that Muslims should kill Americans, including civilians, wherever they can be found.

March 1998
Brussels police arrest seven members of the Armed Islamic Group and confiscate a cache of explosives.

May 1998
Bin Laden publishes a declaration of Jihad against the United States in the London-based Al-Quds al-Arabia.

Bin Laden holds a press conference in Khost, Afghanistan, where he reiterates his intentions to kill Americans.

London police arrest eight members of the Armed Islamic Group.

June 8, 1998

U.S. Attorney Mary Jo White indicts Usama bin Laden for running *al-Qaida* and for the organization's training of tribesmen who killed 13 U.S. soldiers in Somalia in 1993. Two months before the embassy bombings would occur, the indictment is sealed. It is not made public until five months later.[139]

August 2, 1998

Mohamed Odeh and several *al-Qaida* operatives, including the Kenyan cell leader, meet in Nairobi, Kenya. They are told that all *al-Qaida* operatives must leave Kenya by August 6, 1998.

August 5, 1998

Newspapers publish a statement by the Egyptian Jihad stating that it would retaliate for the U.S. involvement in the extradition of its members from Albania to Egypt.

August 7, 1998

Two truck bombs explode minutes apart outside the U.S. embassies in Kenya and Tanzania, killing 234 people, 12 of them American, and wounding over 5,000 others.

Mohammed Odeh is arrested in Pakistan with a false passport. He is later extradited to Kenya.[140]

August 16, 1998

Kenya turns Mohamed Odeh over to the FBI. Odeh admits he is an active member of *al-Qaida* and that *al-Qaida* is responsible for the African Embassy bombings.

August 20, 1998

In retaliation for the East African embassy bombings, the United States responds with simultaneous cruise missile attacks on several bases inside Afghanistan and on a suspected bin Laden chemical facility in Sudan.

The attacks are followed with an amendment to President Bill Clinton's Executive Order 12947. The amended Executive Order, under the authority of the International Emergency Economic Powers Act (50 U.S.C. 1701 et seq.), blocks all property and interests in property and prohibits any transactions with bin Laden and other terrorists named.

August 27, 1998

Mohamed Rashed Daoud Al-Owhali is brought to the United States and arrested on charges connected with the Nairobi embassy bombing.[141]

---

[139] "The U.S. Embassy Bombings Trial Timeline," www.CNN.com.
[140] Ismail Khan Peshawar, "Bin Laden's Life Saved by Doctor," *Sunday Times* (London), April 9, 2000.
[141] FBI, Press Release, August 28, 1998, available at www.fbi.gov/pressrm/pressrel/pressrel98.htm.

August 28, 1998
Mohamed Odeh is brought to the United States and arrested on charges connected with the Nairobi embassy bombing.[142]

September 18, 1998
U.S. intelligence thwarts a bomb attack against the American embassy in Kampala, Uganda. Twenty suspects are arrested including Sheik Abdul Abdullah Amin, Omar Ahmed Mandela, and Mohamed Gulam Kabba.[143]

September 23, 1998
British authorities arrest seven suspected members of *al-Qaida* in London.[144]

September 24, 1998
As many as 100 German police and paramilitary troops are deployed to protect the U.S. consulate in Hamburg against a reported *al-Qaida* threat.[145]

November 4, 1998
The United States Attorney General indicts bin Laden along with Muhammad Aref, *al-Qaida's* military commander, on a total of 224 counts of murder in connection with the U.S. embassy bombings in East Africa.

January 19, 1999
The New Delhi Police arrest Syed Abu Nasir, a Bangladeshi national, who is allegedly a member of the Lashkar-e-Toiba (the Army of the Pure), the armed wing of the Pakistan-based Markaz Dawa Al Irshad (Center For Preaching), recovering two kilograms of RDX explosives and some detonators. He claims to have entered India from Pakistan via Bangladesh in October 1998, along with six other men—four from Egypt and one each from Sudan and Myanmar—to organize explosions outside the U.S. consulates in Calcutta and Chennai around January 26, 1999.

February 1999
Uruguayan authorities arrest three supposed *al-Qaida* associates in the border town of Chuy. They were entering the country from Brazil with forged Malaysian passports and were reportedly planning to board a flight to Paris or London. A fourth suspect escaped customs officials at the border.[146]

---

[142] *Ibid.*

[143] Michael Grunwald, "CIA Helps Thwart Bomb Plot Against Embassy in Uganda," *Seattle Times*, September 25, 1998.

[144] Steve Macko, "British Authorities Pick Up More Suspected Transnational Terrorists," EmergencyNet News—ERRI, September 24, 1998.

[145] "Terror Threat on Hamburg, Germany Consulate," EmergencyNet News—ERRI, September 24, 1998.

[146] "Uruguayans Arrest bin Laden Associate," B'nai B'rith, *op. cit.*

February 13, 1999

The Taliban announces that bin Laden has disappeared from his Afghan camp. The disappearance of bin Laden places the U.S. government in a state of alert and sparks an intensive international search by U.S. intelligence agencies.

April 18, 1999

An Egyptian military court sentenced nine of the 107 defendants in the "Returnees from Afghanistan" case to death, others receiving varying sentences. Twenty of the defendants were acquitted. Among those sentenced to death *in absentia* were Ayman and Mohammed Zawahiri.[147]

April 30, 1999

A London-based newspaper, *The Independent*, cites U.S. State Department sources saying bin Laden is seeking to relocate to Somalia.

May 3, 1999

Somali warlord Hussein Mohammad Aideed refutes claims that bin Laden has a base in his area of control. However, he does not rule out the possibility that bin Laden operatives may be in the Gedo region of southern Somalia.

June 7, 1999

The FBI adds Usama bin Laden to the 10 Most Wanted list.

June 10,1999

In an interview broadcast on Qatari television, bin Laden calls for war against Israel and the United States. Bin Laden is described as depressed, believing that he should have been "martyred" in Afghanistan fighting the Soviet Union.[148]

July 7, 1999

President Bill Clinton imposes sanctions against the Taliban for harboring bin Laden. The sanctions prohibit trade or transactions with the Taliban and freezes any Taliban assets in U.S. jurisdiction.

July 8, 1999

The Taliban confirms that bin Laden has relocated his base of operations to Farmihadda, Afghanistan, near the Pakistani border. This confirmation comes after locals report seeing bin Laden and *al-Qaida* operatives in the area.

July 17, 1999

The Albanian government deports three suspected operatives. The three suspects consisted of two Syrians and an Iraqi.

---

[147] Simon Apiku, "Egyptian Military Tribunal Slams Militants," *Middle East Times*, April 25, 1999.
[148] "Bin Laden Renews Calls for Terror Attacks on Americans," *Deutsche Presse-Agentur*, June 10, 1999.

July 30, 1999

The Taliban publicly reinforces its position to offer Usama bin Laden safe haven, calling him a guest of the Afghan people since the "Jihad against the Soviet forces."

October 5, 1999

South African authorities arrest Khalfan Khamis Mohamed in Cape Town.[149]

October 13, 1999

Mahrez Hamduni, an aide to Usama bin Laden, is arrested by Interpol at Istanbul's international airport. He is carrying a Bosnian passport.

The Taliban arrests Khalil al-Deek and a young Jordanian man, Abu al-Mubtasim, on charges of spying on bin Laden for a "foreign country."

October 16, 1999

The United Nations Security Council imposes sanctions on the Taliban until bin Laden is expelled from their borders. The sanctions, to take effect in 30 days, prohibit any transactions between member states and the Taliban.

October 20, 1999

Two members of an eight-man *al-Qaida* "commando" unit are arrested in Turkey after crossing the border from Iran. One suspect confirms the unit's connection to Usama bin Laden and informs Turkish officials of their plan to attack the conference on European Cooperation and Security. The at-large suspects consist of four Kurds and two Algerians.

November 19, 1999

Afghan clerics who support the Northern Alliance against the Taliban issued a fatwa that it was legal under Islamic Sharia law to kill Usama bin Laden.[150]

December, 1999

The U.S. government obtains from Jordan copies of a CD-ROM containing a six-volume manual allegedly used by bin Laden to train *al-Qaida* recruits in Afghanistan. The manual was found on a group of men arrested in Jordan for allegedly planning New Year's attacks in Israel and Jordan. The manual is described as being a "briefing book on 'how to conduct terror'."[151]

December 14, 1999

Ahmed Ressam is arrested in Port Angeles, Washington, for possession of explosive materials. His vehicle contained 110 pounds of urea, fourteen pounds of sulfate, and four homemade timers. At the time of his arrest, Ressam held airplane tickets to London. Ressam, an Algerian, has ties to the GIA.

[149] Weiser, "Man Charged," *op. cit.*
[150] "Afghan Clerics Issue bin Laden Fatwa," BBC, November 19, 1999.
[151] Jack Kelley, "CD-ROM Contains Guide for Terrorists," *USA Today*, September 18, 2000, p. 1A.

December 15, 1999

Jordanian officials arrest 13 suspected terrorists, accusing them of planning attacks against the Radisson Hotel in Amman, three tourist sites frequented by Israelis and Westerners, and two border crossings into Israel. Mohammed Hussein Zein-al-Abideen flees from Pakistan to Afghanistan shortly afterwards.[152]

December 19, 1999

Lucia Garofalo, a Canadian citizen, and Bouabide Chamchi, an Algerian national, are arrested at the Quebec/Vermont border after traces of explosives are found on the fender of their vehicle. Chamchi holds a false passport. The vehicle and cellular phone were both registered to Garofalo and Brahim Mahdi, a member of the Algerian Islamic League. The Algerian Islamic League is headed by Mourad Dhina, an international arms dealer and financier of terrorist organizations.

December 30, 1999

A New York terrorism task force detains Abdel Ghani after finding his telephone number and address on Ahmed Ressam. Ghani traveled from New York to Seattle using the alias Eduardo Rocha.

January 23, 2000

U.S. Department of Justice files documents outlining the structure of *al-Qaida*. It provides information concerning fundraising, how weapons are obtained, and the procurement of passports.

January 28, 2000

Mohambedou Ould Slahi is arrested in Nouakchott, Mauritania, upon request of the United States. He is suspected of being the head of the Montreal terrorist cell conspiring to attack the United States. Slahi is the brother-in-law or one of *al-Qaida*'s top lieutenants.

February 8, 2000

The Royal Canadian Mounted Police dispatch a team of detectives to Europe to question Hamid Aich and Fateh Kamel for their involvement in the New Years Eve bombing conspiracy.

February 22, 2000

Bin Laden is reported to be in deteriorating health and preparing to turn over control of *al-Qaida* to al-Zawahiri. Experts state that this might be a ruse for bin Laden to take a more back-seat role as U.S. pressure on *al-Qaida* and Afghanistan increases.[153]

---

[152] Risen, "Foiled Terror Plot," *op. cit.*
[153] Mohamad Bazzi, "Bin Laden May Be Ready to Turn over Terrorist Network to Aide," *Houston Chronicle*, February 22, 2000.

March, 2000

A planned visit by President Clinton to a village in Bangladesh is called off based on a terrorist threat possibly linked to bin Laden.[154]

March 17, 2000

News reports state that bin Laden is dying of kidney failure.[155]

March 28, 2000

Jordan indicts 28 Arabs linked to bin Laden on charges related to planned attacks against an American hotel and three tourist sites frequented by Israelis and Westerners. Fifteen of the suspects have been in custody since December 1999, while the remaining 13 were indicted *in absentia* and may be hiding in Pakistan, Afghanistan, Britain, Lebanon, and Syria.[156]

April 2, 2000

Ahmed Abdullah is arrested in Pakistan.

April 2, 2000

The Pristina, Kosovo, headquarters of the Saudi Joint Relief Committee is raided by Italian paramilitary members of the United Missions in Kosovo, after a tip-off from U.S. intelligence sources that the group was linked to bin Laden.[157]

April 9, 2000

Bin Laden is reported to be recovering in Afghanistan from treatment for kidney and liver disease. Witnesses describe him as gaunt, weak, depressed, and undergoing dialysis treatment.[158]

May, 2000

Attorney General Janet Reno secretly authorizes federal prosecutors to seek the death penalty against Mohamed Rashed Daoud al-Owhali for his involvement in the U.S. Embassy bombings.[159]

May 23, 2000

Jamal Tahrawi is arrested in Amman.[160]

---

[154] "Report on bin Laden Altered Clinton Plan," *New York Times*, March 22, 2000, p. 18.
[155] Katherine Butler, "Bin Laden Said to be Dying of Kidney Failure," *The Independent* (London), March 17, 2000, p. 18.
[156] "Jordan Indicts 28 in Terror Conspiracy Linked to bin Laden," *New York Times*, March 29, 2000, p. A5.
[157] Christian Jennings, "NATO Claims bin Laden Planned Pristina Attacks," *The Scotsman* (London), April 5, 2000, p. 10.
[158] Peshawar, "Bin Laden's Life Saved by Doctor," *op. cit.*
[159] Benjamin Weiser, "U.S. to Seek Death Penalty in Bombings," *New York Times*, May 10, 2000, p. B1.
[160] *Journal Sentinel* Wire Reports, May 23, 2000.

June 1, 2000
Group led by Nabil Okal arrested in the West Bank.[161]

Mid-June, 2000
Pakistani officials claim that the Taliban has shut down *al-Qaida* training camps in Afghanistan.[162]

June 24, 2000
Abdel Salem Boulanouar is arrested in Paris after being deported from the Philippines.[163]

June 30, 2000
Eight alleged *al-Qaida* members are convicted in a Lebanese military court with prison sentences ranging from two weeks to five years. The charges range from conspiracy to commiting terrorism to forgery.[164]

July 5, 2000
Mohamed Zeki Mahjoub arrested in Toronto.[165]

Summer, 2000
Approximately sixty members of *al-Qaida*, led by Omar Abdul Hakim Abu Muasab Soori, defect from the organization to form a separate, pro-Taliban group. This comes after the Taliban exerts more control over the operations of *al-Qaida* and attempts to isolate bin Laden. Additionally, at least two separate assassination attempts against bin Laden are prevented when the Taliban captures the assassins. These actions increase bin Laden's concern for his safety.[166]

September 2000
A Jordanian military court convicted 22 of the 28 men charged with the 1999 bombing plot and sentenced 6 to death.

September 15, 2000
The United States puts the Islamic Movement of Uzbekistan on its terrorist list citing connections with bin Laden and *al-Qaida*.[167]

---

[161] Arieh O'Sullivan, "Bin Laden Ring Planned Mass Terror Campaign: Israeli, PA Security Forces Arrest 23 Members," *Jerusalem Post*, August 23, 2000.
[162] Ismail Khan, "Taliban Claims Bin Laden has Lost Terrorist Lairs," *Sunday Times* (London), June 18, 2000.
[163] McNeil, Jr., "French Hold Suspected Terrorist," *op. cit.*
[164] "Terror Suspect's Colleagues Convicted: 8 Followers of bin Laden Sentenced in Attack Plans," *Ottawa Citizen*, July 1, 2000.
[165] Almira Elghwaby, Jim Rankin, and Allan Thompson, "Toronto Man Linked to Terrorism," *Toronto Star*, July 7, 2000.
[166] Julian West, "Bin Laden in Fear of His Life After Key Aides Defect," *Sunday Telegraph* (London), July 30, 2000, p. 28.
[167] Judith Miller, "US Puts Uzbek Group on Its Terror List," *New York Times*, September 15, 2000.

September 18, 2000

Reports surface that U.S. intelligence has obtained bin Laden's "Encyclopedia," which contains such information as how to recruit followers and how to conduct operations.[168]

September 22, 2000

In a videotape broadcast on Qatari television, bin Laden vows to free Sheikh Omar Abdel Rahman. The authenticity of the tape is questioned, however, when the Taliban issues a statement stating that bin Laden is not allowed to make statements against other countries while in Afghanistan and is prevented access to communications equipment.[169]

October 5, 2000

The USS *Cole* is attacked in a suicide bombing, which kills 17 and wounds 39 American sailors in Aden harbor, Yemen; *al-Qaida* is suspected of mounting the operation.

October 21, 2000

Abdel-Bari Atwan, editor of the *Al Quds Al-Arabi* newspaper, was reportedly told by a bin Laden associate that *al-Qaida* had been planning to attack Americans in Yemen for two years. The report also stated that bin Laden had married a Yemeni woman a few months before the *Cole* incident, giving him family ties to an important Yemeni tribe.[170]

October 31, 2000

The Jamiat Ulema-e-Islam warns that it will retaliate against the United States if Afghanistan or Usama bin Laden is attacked by the United States.[171]

November 1, 2000

Mamdouh Mahmud Salim stabbed one prison guard in the eye and sprayed others with irritants during a failed escape from the Metropolitan Correctional Center in Manhattan.[172]

December 19, 2000

The United Nations Security Council passes Resolution 1333, banning all military assistance to the Taliban in an effort to close terrorist camps in Afghanistan and to hand over Usama bin Laden to appropriate authorities.[173]

---

[168] Kelley, "CD-ROM," *op. cit.*

[169] David Ensor and Jonathan D. Austin, "Authenticity of Bin Laden Videotape Questioned," CNN.com, September 22, 2000. Available at www.cnn.com/2000/world/meast/09/22/osama.bin.laden/.

[170] "Bin Laden 'Groomed Yemen Ties for Two Years'," *Gulf News* (Dubai), October 21, 2000.

[171] "JUI Warns Washington," *Gulf News, op.cit.*

[172] "Former Top Aide to Bin Laden Allegedly Planned Dramatic Escape," CNN, December 21, 2000.

[173] UNSC Resolution 1333 (2000).

December 20, 2000

A United States federal grand jury indicts five more people for the 1998 East African embassy bombings. Four of the five—Saif Al Adel, Mushin Musa Matwalli Atwah, Ahmed Mohammed Hamed Ali, and Anas Al Liby—face up to life in prison for their involvement. While Abdullah Ahmed Abdullah faces the death penalty for playing a direct role. All men are currently at large. [174]

December 28, 2000

German police arrest four suspected members of al-Qaida in Frankfurt. The police uncovered a large amount of weapons and explosives. Out of the four, it was reported that one was an Algerian, one was a French national, and the other two were Iraqi.[175] Separately, Mamdouh Mahmud Salim was indicted in New York for attempted murder due to his November 2000 attack on a federal prison guard.[176]

January 3, 2001

Jury selection begins at the Southern District Court of New York in the trial of Mohamed Rashed D. al-Owhali, Khalfan Khamis Mohamed, Mohamed Sadeek Odeh, and Wadih el Hage.

January 10, 2001

Eight people are arrested in Kenya with ties to bin Laden and *al-Qaida*.[177]

January 22, 2001

Reports that the Pakistani government had frozen bin Laden's assets and closed the offices of the Taliban and Ariana Afghan Airlines within the country to comply with the UN sanctions were denied by Pakistani officials.[178]

February 6, 2001

Jamal Al-Fadhl, known only as CS-1 prior to taking the stand, testifies as the prosecution's first witness in the East African embassy bombings case at the Southern District Court of New York. He gives a detailed account into the workings of *al-Qaida*.

February 7, 2001

The trial begins in Paris of two dozen Islamic militants linked to the Groupe Roubaix that terrorized the group's namesake city in Northern France. Seven are being tried *in absentia*, including Ahmed Ressam, who is in custody in the United States for trying to smuggle explosives across the Canadian border into Port Angeles, Washington,3 in late

---

[174] Eggen and Vise, "More Indicted in Embassy Attacks," *op. cit.*

[175] "Germany Arrests Four Islamic Suspects," BBC, December 28, 2000, and "German Police Arrest Suspected Islamic Guerillas," Reuters, December 28, 2000.

[176] "German Police Arrest," Reuters, *op. cit.*

[177] Tony Kago, "Slavery Suspects Linked to Osama Bin Laden," *Nation* (Nairobi), January 23, 2001.

[178] "Islamabad Freezes Bin Laden Assets," *Gulf News* (Dubai), January 22, 2001.

December 1999. Also on trial in Paris is Fateh Kamel; the alleged leader of the group allegedly has ties with *al-Qaida*.[179]

February 14, 2001
Essam al-Ridi, a former business acquitance of bin Laden, testifies for the prosecution at the Southern District Court of New York that bin Laden, with el Hage as the middleman, bought a private plane with the intention of shipping Stinger antiaircraft missiles from Pakistan to the Sudan.[180]

February 18, 2001
Yemeni President Ali Abdullah Saleh announces the arrest of two Yemenis, Mohammed Ahmed al-Ahdal and Ahmed Mohammed Amin, in connection with the October 2000 attack on the USS *Cole*.

February 21, 2001
L'Houssaine Kherchtou begins testimony for the prosecution at the Southern District Court of New York. He identifies Mohammed Sadeek Odeh and Wadih el Hage as members of *al-Qaida*, placing Odeh in Somalia in 1993 and el Hage in Kenya in 1995.[181]

February 26, 2001
At a wedding reception for his son, Usama bin Laden recited a poem celebrating the bombing of the USS *Cole*, according to Saudi newspaper Pan-Arab Al-Hayat.[182]

February 27, 2001
Under cross-examination by el Hage's lawyers at the Southern District Court of New York, Kherchtou contradicts his previous testimony, stating that he cannot be sure that el Hage was a member of *al-Qaida*.[183]

February 28, 2001
FBI Special Agent John Anticev testifies at the Southern District Court of New York that Mohamed Sadeek Odeh, in an interview with him in August 1998, called the Nairobi bombing a "blunder" and regretted the death of many Kenyans. Anticev also stated that Odeh believed that *al-Qaida* carried out the Nairobi attack under Abdullah Ahmed Abdullah, but Odeh was not involved personally.[184]

---

[179] Ganley, "Islamic Militants Trial Begins," *op. cit.*, and Von Derschau, "Defendant: Apartment Was for Meetings," *op. cit.*

[180] Statement by Essam al-Ridi, op. cit., and Deborah Feyerick and Phil Hirschkorn, "Embassy Bombing Defendant Linked to bin Laden," CNN, February 14, 2001.

[181] Statement by prosecution witness L'Houssaine Kherchtou at the Southern District Court in New York on February 21, 2001, and Hirschkorn, "Bin Laden the Focus," *op. cit.*

[182] "Bin Laden Says *Cole* Sailed Slowly to Its Doom—Paper," Reuters, March 1, 2001.

[183] Hirschkorn, "Witness Backtracks," *op. cit.*

[184] John Anticev, Statement, *op. cit.*; Hirschkorn, "Agent," *op. cit.*; and Appleson, "Bin Laden Follower," *op. cit.*

Selected Sources and Bibliography

"Afghan Clerics Issue bin Laden Fatwa," BBC, November 19, 1999.

Yonah Alexander, Middle East Terrorism: Selected Group Profiles (Washington, D.C.: JINSA, 1994).

John Anticev, Sworn Testimony in the Southern District Court of New York on February 28, 2001.

Simon Apiku, "Egyptian Military Tribunal Slams Militants," *Middle East Times*; April 25, 1999.

Simon Apiku, "Wanted: Terrorists Living Abroad," *Middle East Times*, January 27, 1999.

Gail Appleson, "Bin Laden Follower Says Colleagues Did Bombing," Reuters, February 28, 2001.

"An Arrest in Embassy Bombings," *New York Times*, April 3, 2000.

Devlin Barrett, "Terror witness' radioactive revelation," *New York Post*, February 8, 2001.

Mohamad Bazzi, "Bin Laden May Be Ready to Turn over Terrorist Network to Aide," *Houston Chronicle*, February 22, 2000.

"Bin Laden 'Groomed Yemen ties for two years'," *Gulf News* (Dubai); October 21, 2000.

"Bin Laden Renews Calls for Terror Attacks on Americans," *Deutsche Presse-Agentur*, June 10, 1999.

"Bin Laden Said to Get Millions from Wealthy in Gulf," *Boston Globe*, July 7, 1999.

"Bin Laden Says *Cole* Sailed Slowly to Its Doom—Paper," Reuters, March 1, 2001.

John Burns, "Where bin Laden Has Roots, His Mystique Grows," *New York Times*, December 31, 2000.

Katherine Butler, "Bin Laden Said to be Dying of Kidney Failure," *The Independent* (London), March 17, 2000.

Mike Carter, "Feds Link Ressam to Terror Camps," *Seattle Times*, March 9, 2001.

Central Intelligence Agency, "Statement by Director of Central Intelligence George J. Tenet before the Senate Select Committee on Intelligence on The Worldwide Threat in 2000: Global Realities of Our National Security," February 2, 2000, available at www.odci.gov/cia/public_affairs/speeches/dci_speech_020200.html

"Confession Allowed in Terrorist Case," *San Diego Union-Tribune* (Reuters), January 30, 2001.

Jim Dwyer and Greg B. Smith, "Two Plotted Prison Attack for Days," *New York Daily News*, November 3, 2000.

Dan Eggen and David Vise, "More Indicted in Embassy Attacks." *Washington Post*, December 21, 2000.

"Egypt Says Bin Laden Paid Luxor Gunmen," Reuters, May 13, 1999.

"Egypt Sentences 9 to Death in Biggest Trial of Militants Ever," CNN; April 18, 1999.

Egyptian State Information Service, "Wanted: A Call to Combat Terrorism."

Almira Elghwaby, Jim Rankin, and Allan Thompson, "Toronto Man Linked to Terrorism," *Toronto Star*, July 7, 2000.

Michael Ellison, "Mystery man testifies in bin Laden trial," *The Guardian*, February 7, 2001.

Michael Ellison, "Witness tells of dealings with bin-laden," I*rish Times*, February 7, 2001.

Stephen Engelberg, "One Man and a Global Web of Violence," *New York Times*, January 14, 2001.

David Esnor and Jonathan D. Austin, "Authenticity of bin Laden Videotape Questioned." CNN.com, September 22, 2000, available at www.cnn.com/2000/world/meast/09/22/osama.bin.laden/.

David Ensor, Chris Plante, and Peter Bergen, "USS *Cole* Plot Began After Embassy Attacks, Investigator Says," CNN, December 20, 2000.

Jamal Ahmed al-Fadhl, Sworn Testimony in the Southern District Court of New York, February 6 & 7, 2001.

"Fatwa," February 23, 1998 in *al-Quds al-Arabi* (London), www.ict.org/articles/fatwahh.htm.

FBI Most Wanted.

FBI, Press Release, August 28, 1998, available at www.fbi.gov/pressrm/pressrel/pressrel98.htm.

Ben Fenton, "Bin laden wanted to behead the US snake," *Daily Telegraph*, February 8, 2001.

Ben Fenton, "Four on Trial for Embassy Bombings," Daily Telegraph, February 6, 2001.

Deborah Feyerick and Phil Hirschkorn, "Embassy Bombing Defendant Linked to bin Laden," CNN, February 14, 2001.

Deborah Feyerick and Phil Hirschkorn, "Witness Says He Bought Plane, Made Shipments for bin Laden," CNN, February 14, 2001.

"Five More People Indicted in Embassy Bombings Case," CNN, December 20, 2000.

"Former Top Aide to Bin Laden Allegedly Planed Dramatic Escape," CNN, December 21, 2000.

"Fugitive Arrested for Planning Terrorist Attacks," *Milwaukee Journal Sentinel*, May 25, 2000.

Elaine Ganley, "Islamic Militants Trial Begins," Associated Press, February 7, 2001.

"German Police Arrest Suspected Islamic Guerillas," Reuters, December 28, 2000.

"Germany Arrests Four Islamic Suspects," BBC, December 28, 2000.

Peter Grier, "Terrorist trials: Missing someone?," *Christian Science Monitor*, February 8, 2001.

Michael Grunwald, "CIA Helps Thwart Bomb Plot Against Embassy in Uganda," *Seattle Times*, September 25, 1998.

Jailan Halawi "Bin Laden Behind Luxor Massacre?" *Al-Ahram Weekly*, May 20-26, 1999.

"Haled AL Safani, Suspected of Being Connected with Bin Laden, Deported to BH," Radio Banja Luka News (Bosnia), Tuzla Night Owl (Brcko), November 12, 2000.

Tom Hays, "Embassy Bombing Defendants," Associated Press, February 4, 2001.

Phil Hirschkorn, "Agent: Defendant called Kenya attack a 'blunder'," CNN, February 28, 2001.

Phil Hirschkorn, "Bin Laden the Focus of Embassy Bombing Trial," CNN, February 21, 2001.

Phil Hirschkorn, "Witness Backtracks at Embassy Bombings Trial," CNN, February 27, 2001.

Phil Hirschkorn and Deborah Feyerick, "Embassy bombings trial witness says bin laden wanted to buy uranium," CNN, February 7, 2001.

Carola Hoyos, "Embassies Bombed to Drive Out U.S.," *Financial Times*, February 6, 2001.

"Hunting bin Laden: Who is bin Laden?", PBS Frontline (1999).

Zahid Hussain, "Dozen Rebel Groups Wage Unrelenting War Against India," *The Times* (UK), December 28, 2000.

"Islamabad Freezes Bin Laden Assets," *Gulf News* (Dubai), January 22, 2001.

Ahmed Ismail, "Senior Islamist Activist May Be Under Arrest," *Middle East Times*, June 16, 2000.

Christian Jennings, "NATO Claims bin Laden Planned Pristina Attacks," *The Scotsman* (London), April 5, 2000.

David Johnston, "Evidence Is Seen Linking bin Laden to Algerian Group," *New York Times*, January 27, 2000.

"Jordan Indicts 28 in Terror Conspiracy Linked to bin Laden," *New York Times*, March 29, 2000.

Journal Sentinel Wire Reports, May 23, 2000.

"JUI Warns Washington," *Gulf News* (Dubai) October 31, 2000.

Ashif Mohamed Juma, Statements made by prosecution witness under oath in the Southern District Court of New York, on February 14, 2001.

Tony Kago, "Slavery Suspects Linked to Osama Bin Laden, " *Nation* (Nairobi), January 23, 2001.

Mustapha Kamil, "Witness sheds some light on Osama's alleged terror network," *New Straits Times* (Malaysia), February 8, 2001.

Jack Kelley, "CD-ROM Contains Guide for Terrorists," USA Today, September 18, 2000.

Jack Kelley, "Saudi Money Aiding bin Laden: Businessmen Are Financing Front Groups," *USA Today*, October 29, 1999.

Jack Kelley, "Terrorists use web to mount attacks," *Arizona Republic*, February 6, 2001.

Ismail Khan, "Taliban Claims Bin Laden has Lost Terrorist Lairs," *Sunday Times* (London), June 18, 2000.

L'Houssaine Kherchtou, Statement at the Southern District Court in New York on February 21, 2001.

Laura King, "Bin Laden Links Sought Amid Arrests," Associated Press, February 21, 2001.

Andrea Koppel and David Ensor, "Suspect in Alleged U.S. Millennium Plot arrested in Algeria." CNN, December 7, 2000.

Jill Krauss, " First witness testifies in bombing trial," ABC NEWS, February 6, 2001.

"Kuwait Deports Egyptian, Bosnian as Suspected Terrorists," *Gulf News* (Dubai), Reuters, November 11, 2000.

Joe Lauria, "A Wide Plot to Kill Americans Alleged in Embassy Bomb Trial," *Boston Globe*, February 6, 2001.

"Luqsor Massacre: Shedding the Light on the Western Support for Terrorism," *Al Sha'ab Al-Arabi*, Translated by HIPRS, January 1, 1998.

Colum Lynch, "Witness Tells How Bin Laden Group Works," *Washington Post*, February 7, 2001.

Steve Macko, "British Authorities Pick Up More Suspected Transnational Terrorists," EmergencyNet News—ERRI, September 24, 1998.

Scott Macleod, "The Paladin of Jihad," *Time Magazine*, 147; no. 19, (May 6, 1996).

Donald G. McNeil Jr., "French Hold Suspected Terrorist Tied to bin Laden," *New York Times*, June 28, 2000.

Judith Miller, "Dissecting a Terror Plot from Boston to Amman," *New York Times*, January 15, 2001.

Judith Miller, "Killing for the Glory of God, In a Land Far From Home," *New York Times*, January 16, 2001.

Judith Miller, "US Puts Uzbek Group on Its Terror List," *New York Times*, September 15, 2000.

Judith Miller and Sarah Lyall, "Hunting bin Laden's Allies, U.S. Extends Net to Europe," *New York Times*, February 21, 2001.

Claire Moore, "Embassy Bombing Trial Opens Today," ABC NEWS, February 5, 2001.

Stephen Muiruri, "Three Suspects Picked for Filming Embassy," *Daily Nation* (Nairobi); August 22, 1998.

Larry Neumeister, "5 More Indicted in Embassy Bombings." Associated Press, December 21, 2000.

Larry Neumeister, "Millennium Bomb Plotter Cops Plea," Associated Press, March 9, 2001.

"Nigerian Man Agrees to Cooperate in Millennium Terrorist Plot," CNN, March 8, 2001.

"Osama Moves to Tora Bora base in Afghanistan," *Business Recorder* (Pakistan), March 18, 1999.

Arieh O'Sullivan, "Bin Laden Ring Planned Mass Terror Campaign: Israeli, PA Security Forces Arrest 23 Members," *Jerusalem Post*, August 23, 2000.

Ismail Khan Peshawar, "Bin Laden's Life Saved by Doctor," *Sunday Times* (London), April 9, 2000.

"Report on bin Laden Altered Clinton Plan," *New York Times*, March 22, 2000.

Essam Al-Ridi, Sworn testimony at the Southern District Court of New York, February 14, 2001.

James Risen, "Foiled Terror Plot on Tourists Linked to bin Laden Aide," *New York Times*, February 29, 2000.

James Risen and Benjamin Weiser, "U.S. Officials Say Aid for Terrorists Came Through Two Persian Gulf Nations," *New York Times*, July 8, 1999.

Michael Sheridan, "Hostages Trapped in Web of Muslim Terror," *Sunday Times* (London), May 7, 2000.

Greg B. Smith, "I warned of bombing, ex-terrorist says," *Daily News*, February 8, 2001.

Greg B. Smith, "Trial Begins in Bombing of Embassies, " *Daily News*, February 6, 2001.

"Syria Said to Deport Convicted Muslim Militant," *Gulf News* (Dubai), December 4, 2000.

"Terror Suspect's Colleagues Convicted: 8 Followers of Bin Laden Sentenced in Attack Plans," *Ottawa Citizen*, July 1, 2000.

"Terror Threat on Hamburg, Germany Consulate," EmergencyNet News—ERRI; September 24, 1998.

Kenneth R. Timmerman, "This Man Wants You Dead," *Reader's Digest Magazine*, July, 1998, available at www.readersdigest.com/rdmagazine/specfeat/archives/thismandead.htm.

United States v. Usama bin Laden et al., S (7) 98 Cr. 1023 (LBS). Indictment available at http://www.fbi.gov/majcases/eastafrica/summary.htm.

UNSC Resolution 1333 (2000).

"Uruguayans Arrest bin Laden Associate," Report by B'nai B'rith Center for Public Policy, February 1999.

U.S. Department of State, *Fact Sheet: The Charges Against International Terrorist Usama Bin Laden*, available at www.usembassy.state.gov/posts/af1/wwwh0001.html.

U.S. Department of State, *Fact Sheet: Usama bin Ladin*. Released by the Coordinator for Counterterrorism, August 21, 1998.

U.S. Department of State, *Foreign Terrorist Organizations Designations 1999*, October 8, 1999, available at www.state.gov/www/global/terrorism/annual_reports.html.

U.S. Department of State, *Patterns of Global Terrorism*, 1999.

"The U.S. Embassy Bombings Trial Timeline," www.CNN.com.

"US, Yemen Closing in on Top USS *Cole* Suspect-Paper," Reuters, February 10, 2001.

David Usborne, "Bin laden tied to build nuclear bomb," *The Independent*, February 9, 2001.

"USS *Cole* Plot Began After Embassy Attacks, Investigator Says: Suicide Bomber Identified," CNN; December 20, 2000.

David A. Vise and Lorraine Adams, "Bin Laden Weakened, Officials Say," *Washington Post*, March 11, 2000, March 11, 2000.

Verena Von Derschau, "Defendant: Apartment Was for Meetings," Associated Press, February 16, 2001.

Benjamin Weiser, "Ex-Aide to bin Laden Describes Terror Campaign Aimed at U.S.," *New York Times*, February 7, 2001.

Benjamin Weiser, "Man Charged in Bombing of U.S. Embassy in Africa," *New York Times*, October 9, 1999.

Benjamin Weiser, "U.S. to Seek Death Penalty in Bombings," *New York Times*, May 10, 2000.

Julian West, "Bin Laden in Fear of His Life After Key Aides Defect," *Sunday Telegraph* (London), July 30, 2000.

"Witness: I Worked For bin Laden," Associated Press, February 6, 2001.

Appendices

1. Statements and Declarations made by Usama bin Laden

2. Interviews with Usama bin Laden

3. United States Indictments

4. New York Trial Testimony

5. United States Perspectives: Selected Documents

6. United Nations Resolutions

Statements and Declarations made by Usama bin Laden

DECLARATION OF WAR AGAINST THE AMERICANS
OCCUPYING THE LAND OF THE TWO HOLY PLACES*

A Message from Usama bin Muhammad bin Laden unto
his Muslim Brethren all over the world generally,
and in the Arab Peninsula specifically

{Friday, 9/4/1417 A.H (23/8/1996 CE)}

Praise be to Allah, we seek His help and ask for his pardon. We take refuge in Allah from our wrongs and bad deeds. Who ever been guided by Allah will not be misled, and who ever has been misled, he will never be guided. I bear witness that there is no God except Allah, no associates with Him and I bear witness that Muhammad is His slave and messenger.

{O you who believe! be careful of your duty to Allah with the proper care which is due to Him, and do not die unless you are Muslim} (Imraan; 3:102), {O people be careful of your duty to your Lord, Who created you from a single being and created its mate of the same kind and spread from these two, many men and women; and be careful of your duty to Allah , by whom you demand one of another your rights, and (be careful) to the ties of kinship; surely Allah ever watches over you} (An Nisa; 4:1), {O you who believe! be careful of your duty to Allah and speak the right word; He will put your deeds into a right state for you, and forgive you your faults; and who ever obeys Allah and his Apostle, he indeed achieve a mighty success} (Al Ahzab; 33:7071).

Praise be to Allah, reporting the saying of the prophet Shu'aib: {I desire nothing but reform so far as I am able, and with non but Allah is the direction of my affair to the right and successful path; on him do I rely and to him do I turn} (Hud; 11:88). Praise be to Allah, saying: {You are the best of the nations raised up for the benefit of men; you enjoin what is right and forbid the wrong and believe in Allah} (Aal Imraan; 3:110).

Allah's blessing and salutations on His slave and messenger who said. (The people are close to an all-encompassing punishment from Allah if they see the oppressor and fail to restrain him)

It should not be hidden from you that the people of Islam had suffered from aggression, iniquity and injustice imposed on them by the Zionist-Crusaders alliance and their collaborators; to the extent that the Muslims blood became the cheapest and their wealth as loot in the hands of the enemies. Their blood was spilled in Palestine and Iraq. The horrifying pictures of the massacre of Qana, in Lebanon are still fresh in our memory. Massacres in Tajikistan, Burma, Cashmere, Assam, Philippine, Fatani, Ogadin, Somalia, Eritrea, Chechnya and in Bosnia Herzegovina took place, massacres that send shivers in the body and shake the conscience. All of this and the world watch and hear, and not only didn't respond to these atrocities, but also with a

---

* Source: Azzam Publications
http://www.azzam.com/html/articlesdeclaration.htm

clear conspiracy between the USA and its' allies and under the cover of the iniquitous United
Nations, the dispossessed people were even prevented from obtaining arms to defend themselves.

The people of Islam awakened and realized that they are the main target for the
aggression of the Zionist-Crusaders alliance. All false claims and propaganda about "Human
Rights" were hammered down and exposed by the massacres that took place against the Muslims
in every part of the world. The latest and the greatest of these aggressions, incurred by the
Muslims since the death of the Prophet (ALLAH'S BLESSING AND SALUTATIONS ON
HIM) is the occupation of the land of the two Holy Places the foundation of the house of Islam,
the place of the revelation, the source of the message and the place of the noble Ka'ba, the Qiblah
of all Muslims by the armies of the American Crusaders and their allies. (We bemoan this and
can only say: "No power and power acquiring except through Allah").

Under the present circumstances, and under the banner of the blessed awakening which is
sweeping the world in general and the Islamic world in particular, I meet with you today. And
after a long absence, imposed on the scholars (Ulama) and callers (Da'ees) of Islam by the
iniquitous crusaders movement under the leadership of the USA; who fears that they, the
scholars and callers of Islam, will instigate the Ummah of Islam against its' enemies as their
ancestor scholars may Allah be pleased with them like Ibn Taymiyyah and Al'iz Ibn Abdes
Salaam did. And therefore the Zionist-Crusader alliance resorted to killing and arresting the
truthful Ulama and the working Da'ees (We are not praising or sanctifying them; Allah sanctify
whom He pleased). They killed the Mujahid Sheikh Abdullah Azzaam, and they arrested the
Mujahid Sheikh Ahmad Yaseen and the Mujahid Sheikh Omar Abdur Rahman (in America).

By orders from the USA they also arrested a large number of scholars, Da'ees and young
people in the land of the two Holy Places among them the prominent Sheikh Salman Al Oud'a
and Sheikh Safar Al Hawali and their brothers;(We bemoan this and can only say: "No power
and power acquiring except through Allah"). We, myself and my group, have suffered some of
this injustice ourselves; we have been prevented from addressing the Muslims. We have been
pursued in Pakistan, Sudan and Afghanistan, hence this long absence on my part. But by the
Grace of Allah, a safe base is now available in the high Hindukush mountains in Khurasan ;
whereby the Grace of Allah the largest infidel military force of the world was destroyed. And the
myth of the super power was withered in front of the Mujahideen cries of Allah u Akbar (God is
greater).

Today we work from the same mountains to lift the iniquity that had been imposed on the
Ummah by the Zionist-Crusader alliance, particularly after they have occupied the blessed land
around Jerusalem, route of the journey of the Prophet (ALLAH'S BLESSING AND
SALUTATIONS ON HIM) and the land of the two Holy Places. We ask Allah to bestow us with
victory, He is our Patron and He is the Most Capable. From here, today we begin the work,
talking and discussing the ways of correcting what had happened to the Islamic world in general,
and the Land of the two Holy Places in particular. We wish to study the means that we could
follow to return the situation to its' normal path. And to return to the people their own rights,
particularly after the large damages and the great aggression on the life and the religion of the

2

people. An injustice that had affected every section and group of the people; the civilians, military and security men, government officials and merchants, the young and the old people as well as schools and university students. Hundred of thousands of the unemployed graduates, who became the widest section of the society, were also affected.

Injustice had affected the people of the industry and agriculture. It affected the people of the rural and urban areas. And almost every body complain about something. The situation at the land of the two Holy places became like a huge volcano at the verge of eruption that would destroy the Kufr and the corruption and its' sources. The explosion at Riyadh and Al Khobar is a warning of this volcanic eruption emerging as a result of the sever oppression, suffering, excessive iniquity, humiliation and poverty.

People are fully concerned about their every day livings; every body talks about the deterioration of the economy, inflation, ever increasing debts and jails full of prisoners. Government employees with limited income talk about debts of ten thousands and hundred thousands of Saudi Riyals. They complain that the value of the Riyal is greatly and continuously deteriorating among most of the main currencies. Great merchants and contractors speak about hundreds and thousands of million Riyals owed to them by the government. More than three hundred forty billions of Riyal owed by the government to the people in addition to the daily accumulated interest, let alone the foreign debt. People wonder whether we are the largest oil exporting country?! They even believe that this situation is a curse put on them by Allah for not objecting to the oppressive and illegitimate behavior and measures of the ruling regime:

Ignoring the divine Shari'ah law; depriving people of their legitimate rights; allowing the American to occupy the land of the two Holy Places; imprisonment, unjustly, of the sincere scholars. The honorable Ulamah and scholars as well as merchants, economists and eminent people of the country were all alerted by this disastrous situation.

Quick efforts were made by each group to contain and to correct the situation. All agreed that the country is heading toward a great catastrophe, the depth of which is not known except by Allah. One big merchant commented: " the king is leading the state into `sixty-six' folded disaster", (We bemoan this and can only say: "No power and power acquiring except through Allah"). Numerous princes share with the people their feelings, privately expressing their concerns and objecting to the corruption, repression and the intimidation taking place in the country. But the competition between influential princes for personal gains and interest had destroyed the country. Through its course of actions the regime has torn off its legitimacy:

(1) Suspension of the Islamic Shari'ah law and exchanging it with man made civil law. The regime entered into a bloody confrontation with the truthful Ulamah and the righteous youths (we sanctify nobody; Allah sanctify Whom He pleaseth).

(2) The inability of the regime to protect the country, and allowing the enemy of the Ummah the American crusader forces to occupy the land for the longest of years. The crusader forces became the main cause of our disastrous condition, particularly in the economical aspect of it due

to the unjustified heavy spending on these forces. As a result of the policy imposed on the country, especially in the field of oil industry where production is restricted or expanded and prices are fixed to suit the American economy ignoring the economy of the country. Expensive deals were imposed on the country to purchase arms. People asking what is the justification for the very existence of the regime then?

Quick efforts were made by individuals and by different groups of the society to contain the situation and to prevent the danger. They advised the government both privately and openly; they send letters and poems, reports after reports, reminders after reminders, they explored every avenue and enlist every influential man in their movement of reform and correction. They wrote with style of passion, diplomacy and wisdom asking for corrective measures and repentance from the "great wrong doings and corruption " that had engulfed even the basic principles of the religion and the legitimate rights of the people.

But to our deepest regret the regime refused to listen to the people accusing them of being ridiculous and imbecile. The matter got worse as previous wrong doings were followed by mischief's of greater magnitudes. All of this taking place in the land of the two Holy Places! It is no longer possible to be quiet. It is not acceptable to give a blind eye to this matter.

As the extent of these infringements reached the highest of levels and turned into demolishing forces threatening the very existence of the Islamic principles, a group of scholars who can take no more supported by hundreds of retired officials, merchants, prominent and educated people wrote to the King asking for implementation of the corrective measures. In 1411 A.H. (May 1991), at the time of the gulf war, a letter, the famous letter of Shawwaal, with over four hundred signatures was send to the king demanding the lift of oppression and the implementation of corrective actions. The king humiliated those people and choose to ignore the content of their letter; and the very bad situation of the country became even worse. People, however, tried again and send more letters and petitions. One particular report, the glorious Memorandum Of Advice, was handed over to the king on Muharram, 1413 A.H (July 1992), which tackled the problem pointed out the illness and prescribed the medicine in an original, righteous and scientific style. It described the gaps and the shortcoming in the philosophy of the regime and suggested the required course of action and remedy. The report gave a description of:

(1). The intimidation and harassment suffered by the leaders of the society, the scholars, heads of tribes, merchants, academic teachers and other eminent individuals;

(2). The situation of the law within the country and the arbitrary declaration of what is Halal and Haram (lawful and unlawful) regardless of the Shari'ah as instituted by Allah;

(3). The state of the press and the media which became a tool of truth-hiding and misinformation; the media carried out the plan of the enemy of idolizing cult of certain personalities and spreading scandals among the believers to repel the people away from their religion, as Allah, the Exalted said: {surely as for those who love that scandal should circulate

between the believers, they shall have a grievous chastisement in this world and in the here after}
(An Noor, 24:19).

(4). Abuse and confiscation of human rights;

(5). The financial and the economical situation of the country and the frightening future in the
view of the enormous amount of debts and interest owed by the government; this is at the time
when the wealth of the Ummah being wasted to satisfy personal desires of certain individuals!!
while imposing more custom duties and taxes on the nation. (the prophet said about the woman
who committed adultery: "She repented in such a way sufficient to bring forgiveness to a custom
collector!!").,

(6). The miserable situation of the social services and infrastructure especially the water service
and supply , the basic requirement of life.,

(7). The state of the ill trained and ill-prepared army and the impotence of its commander in
chief despite the incredible amount of money that has been spent on the army. The gulf war
clearly exposed the situation.,

(8). Shari'a law was suspended and man made law was used instead.,

(9). And as far as the foreign policy is concerned the report exposed not only how this policy has
disregarded the Islamic issues and ignored the Muslims, but also how help and support were
provided to the enemy against the Muslims; the cases of Gaza Ariha and the communist in the
south of Yemen are still fresh in the memory, and more can be said.

As stated by the people of knowledge, it is not a secret that to use man made law instead
of the Shari'a and to support the infidels against the Muslims is one of the ten "voiders" that
would strip a person from his Islamic status (turn a Muslim into a Mushrik, non believer status).
The All Mighty said: {and whoever did not judge by what Allah revealed, those are the
unbelievers} (Al Ma'ida; 5:44), and {but no! by your Lord! they do not believe (in reality) until
they make you a judge of that which has become a matter of disagreement among them, and then
do not find the slightest misgiving in their hearts as to what you have decided and submit with
entire submission} (An Nissa; 4:65).

In spite of the fact that the report was written with soft words and very diplomatic style,
reminding of Allah, giving truthful sincere advice, and despite of the importance of advice in
Islam being absolutely essential for those in charge of the people and the large number who
signed this document as well as their supporters, all of that was not an intercession for the
Memorandum . Its' content was rejected and those who signed it and their sympathizers were
ridiculed, prevented from travel, punished and even jailed. Therefore it is very clear that the
advocates of correction and reform movement were very keen on using peaceful means in order
to protect the unity of the country and to prevent blood shed. Why is it then the regime closed all
peaceful routes and pushed the people toward armed actions?!! which is the only choice left for

5

them to implement righteousness and justice. To whose benefit does prince Sultan and prince Nayeff push the country into a civil war that will destroy everything? and why consulting those who ignites internal feuds, playing the people against each other and instigate the policemen, the sons of the nation, to abort the reform movement. While leaving in peace and security such traitors who implement the policy of the enemy in order to bleed the financial and the human resources of the Ummah, and leaving the main enemy in the area the American Zionist alliance enjoy peace and security?! The advisor (Zaki Badr, the Egyptian ex-minister of the interior) to prince Nayeff minister of interior was not acceptable even to his own country; he was sacked from his position there due to the filthy attitude and the aggression he exercised on his own people, yet he was warmly welcomed by prince Nayeff to assist in sins and aggressions. He unjustly filled the prisons with the best sons of this Ummah and caused miseries to their mothers. Does the regime want to play the civilians against their military personnel and vice versa, like what had happened in some of the neighboring countries?!! No doubts this is the policy of the American-Israeli alliance as they are the first to benefit from this situation.

But with the grace of Allah, the majority of the nation, both civilians and military individuals are aware of the wicked plan. They refused to be played against each others and to be used by the regime as a tool to carry out the policy of the American-Israeli alliance through their agent in our country: the Saudi regime. Therefore every one agreed that the situation can not be rectified (the shadow cannot be straighten when its' source, the rod, is not straight either) unless the root of the problem is tackled. Hence it is essential to hit the main enemy who divided the Ummah into small and little countries and pushed it, for the last few decades, into a state of confusion. The Zionist-Crusader alliance moves quickly to contain and abort any "corrective movement" appearing in the Islamic countries. Different means and methods are used to achieve their target; on occasion the "movement" is dragged into an armed struggle at a predetermined unfavorable time and place. Sometime officials from the Ministry of Interior, who are also graduates of the colleges of the Shari'ah, are leashed out to mislead and confuse the nation and the Ummah (by wrong Fatwas) and to circulate false information about the movement. At other occasions some righteous people were tricked into a war of words against the Ulama and the leaders of the movement, wasting the energy of the nation in discussing minor issues and ignoring the main one that is the unification of the people under the divine law of Allah. In the shadow of these discussions and arguments truthfulness is covered by the falsehood, and personal feuds and partisanship created among the people increasing the division and the weakness of the Ummah; priorities of the Islamic work are lost while the blasphemy and polytheism continue its grip and control over the Ummah. We should be alert to these atrocious plans carried out by the Ministry of Interior. The right answer is to follow what have been decided by the people of knowledge, as was said by Ibn Taymiyyah (Allah's mercy upon him): "people of Islam should join forces and support each other to get rid of the main "Kufr" who is controlling the countries of the Islamic world, even to bear the lesser damage to get rid of the major one, that is the great Kufr".

If there are more than one duty to be carried out, then the most important one should receive priority. Clearly after Belief (Imaan) there is no more important duty than pushing the American enemy out of the holy land. No other priority, except Belief, could be considered

6

before it; the people of knowledge, Ibn Taymiyyah, stated: "to fight in defense of religion and Belief is a collective duty; there is no other duty after Belief than fighting the enemy who is corrupting the life and the religion. There is no preconditions for this duty and the enemy should be fought with one best abilities. (ref: supplement of Fatawa). If it is not possible to push back the enemy except by the collective movement of the Muslim people, then there is a duty on the Muslims to ignore the minor differences among themselves; the ill effect of ignoring these differences, at a given period of time, is much less than the ill effect of the occupation of the Muslims' land by the main Kufr. Ibn Taymiyyah had explained this issue and emphasized the importance of dealing with the major threat on the expense of the minor one. He described the situation of the Muslims and the Mujahideen and stated that even the military personnel who are not practicing Islam are not exempted from the duty of Jihad against the enemy.

Ibn Taymiyyah , after mentioning the Moguls (Tatar) and their behavior in changing the law of Allah, stated that: the ultimate aim of pleasing Allah, raising His word, instituting His religion and obeying His messenger (ALLAH'S BLESSING AND SALUTATIONS ON HIM) is to fight the enemy, in every aspects and in a complete manner; if the danger to the religion from not fighting is greater than that of fighting, then it is a duty to fight them even if the intention of some of the fighter is not pure i.e. . fighting for the sake of leadership (personal gain) or if they do not observe some of the rules and commandments of Islam. To repel the greatest of the two dangers on the expense of the lesser one is an Islamic principle which should be observed. It was the tradition of the people of the Sunnah (Ahlul Sunnah) to join and invade fight with the righteous and non righteous men. Allah may support this religion by righteous and non righteous people as told by the prophet (ALLAH'S BLESSING AND SALUTATIONS ON HIM). If it is not possible to fight except with the help of non righteous military personnel and commanders, then there are two possibilities: either fighting will be ignored and the others, who are the great danger to this life and religion, will take control; or to fight with the help of non righteous rulers and therefore repelling the greatest of the two dangers and implementing most, though not all, of the Islamic laws. The latter option is the right duty to be carried out in these circumstances and in many other similar situation. In fact many of the fights and conquests that took place after the time of Rashidoon, the guided Imams, were of this type. (majmoo' al Fatawa, 26/506). No one, not even a blind or a deaf person , can deny the presence of the widely spread mischief's or the prevalence of the great sins that had reached the grievous iniquity of polytheism and to share with Allah in His sole right of sovereignty and making of the law. The All Mighty stated: {And when Luqman said to his son while he admonish him: O my son! do not associate ought with Allah; most surely polytheism is a grievous iniquity} (Luqman; 31:13). Man fabricated laws were put forward permitting what has been forbidden by Allah such as usury (Riba) and other matters. Banks dealing in usury are competing, for lands, with the two Holy Places and declaring war against Allah by disobeying His order {Allah has allowed trading and forbidden usury} (Baqarah; 2:275). All this taking place at the vicinity of the Holy Mosque in the Holy Land! Allah (SWT) stated in His Holy Book a unique promise (that had not been promised to any other sinner) to the Muslims who deals in usury: {O you who believe! Be careful of your duty to Allah and relinquish what remains (due) from usury, if you are believers * But if you do (it) not, then be appraised of WAR from Allah and His Apostle} (Baqarah; 2:278279). This is for the "Muslim" who deals in usury (believing that it is a sin), what is it then to the person who make himself a partner and equal to Allah, legalizing (usury and other sins) what has been forbidden by Allah. Despite of all of the above we see the government misled and dragged some of the righteous Ulamah and Da'ees away from the issue of objecting to the greatest of sins and Kufr. (We bemoan this and can only say: "No power and power acquiring except through Allah").

Under such circumstances, to push the enemy the greatest Kufr out of the country is a prime duty. No other duty after Belief is more important than the duty of had . Utmost effort should be made to prepare and instigate the Ummah against the enemy, the American-Israeli alliance occupying the country of the two Holy Places and the route of the Apostle (Allah's Blessings and Salutations may be on him) to the Furthest Mosque (Al Aqsa Mosque). Also to remind the Muslims not to be engaged in an internal war among themselves, as that will have grieve consequences namely:

(1) Consumption of the Muslims human resources as most casualties and fatalities will be among the Muslims people.

(2) Exhaustion of the economic and financial resources.

(3) Destruction of the country infrastructures

(4) Dissociation of the society

(5) Destruction of the oil industries. The presence of the USA Crusader military forces on land, sea and air of the states of the Islamic Gulf is the greatest danger threatening the largest oil reserve in the world. The existence of these forces in the area will provoke the people of the country and induces aggression on their religion, feelings and prides and push them to take up armed struggle against the invaders occupying the land; therefore spread of the fighting in the region will expose the oil wealth to the danger of being burned up. The economical interest of the States of the Gulf and the land of the two Holy Places will be damaged and even a greater damage will be caused to the economy of the world. I would like here to alert my brothers, the Mujahideen, the sons of the nation, to protect this (oil) wealth and not to include it in the battle as it is a great Islamic wealth and a large economical power essential for the soon to be established Islamic state, by Allah's Permission and Grace. We also warn the aggressors, the USA, against burning this Islamic wealth (a crime which they may commit in order to prevent it, at the end of the war, from falling in the hands of its' legitimate owners and to cause economical damages to the competitors of the USA in Europe or the Far East, particularly Japan which is the major consumer of the oil of the region).

(6) Division of the land of the two Holy Places, and annexing of the northerly part of it by Israel. Dividing the land of the two Holy Places is an essential demand of the Zionist-Crusader alliance. The existence of such a large country with its huge resources under the leadership of the forthcoming Islamic State, by Allah's Grace, represent a serious danger to the very existence of the Zionist state in Palestine. The Nobel Ka'ba, the Qiblah of all Muslims makes the land of the two Holy Places a symbol for the unity of the Islamic world. Moreover, the presence of the

world largest oil reserve makes the land of the two Holy Places an important economical power in the Islamic world. The sons of the two Holy Places are directly related to the life style (Seerah) of their forefathers, the companions, may Allah be pleased with them. They consider the Seerah of their forefathers as a source and an example for reestablishing the greatness of this Ummah and to raise the word of Allah again. Furthermore the presence of a population of fighters in the south of Yemen, fighting in the cause of Allah, is a strategic threat to the Zionist-Crusader alliance in the area. The Prophet (ALLAH'S BLESSING AND SALUTATIONS ON HIM) said: (around twelve thousands will emerge from Aden/Abian helping the cause of Allah and His messenger, they are the best, in the time, between me and them) narrated by Ahmad with a correct trustworthy reference.

(7) An internal war is a great mistake, no matter what reasons are there for it. the presence of the occupier the USA forces will control the outcome of the battle for the benefit of the international Kufr.

I address now my brothers of the security and military forces and the national guards may Allah preserve you hoard for Islam and the Muslims people: O you protectors of unity and guardians of Faith; O you descendent of the ancestors who carried the light (torch) of guidance and spread it all over the world. O you grandsons of Sa'd Ibn Abi Waqqaas , Almothanna Ibn Haritha Ash Shaybani , Alga'ga' Ibn Amroo Al Tammy and those pious companions who fought Jihad alongside them; you competed to join the army and the guard forces with the intention to carry out Jihad in the cause of Allah raising His word and to defend the faith of Islam and the land of the two Holy Places against the invaders and the occupying forces. That is the ultimate level of believing in this religion "Deen". But the regime had reversed these principles and their understanding, humiliating the Ummah and disobeying Allah. Half a century ago the rulers promised the Ummah to regain the first Qiblah, but fifty years later new generation arrived and the promises have been changed; Al Aqsa Mosque handed over to the Zionists and the wounds of the Ummah still bleeding there. At the time when the Ummah has not regained the first Qiblah and the rout of the journey of the Prophet (Allah's Blessings and Salutations may be on him), and despite of all of the above, the Saudi regime had stunt the Ummah in the remaining sanctities, the Holy city of Makka and the mosque of the Prophet (Al Masjid An Nabawy), by calling the Christians army to defend the regime. The crusaders were permitted to be in the land of the two Holy Places. Not surprisingly though, the King himself wore the cross on his chest. The country was widely opened from the north to the south and from east to the west for the crusaders. The land was filled with the military bases of the USA and the allies. The regime became unable to keep control without the help of these bases. You know more than any body else about the size, intention and the danger of the presence of the USA military bases in the area. The regime betrayed the Ummah and joined the Kufr, assisting and helping them against the Muslims. It is well known that this is one of the ten "voiders" of Islam, deeds of de-Islamisation . By opening the Arab peninsula to the crusaders the regime disobeyed and acted against what has been enjoined by the messenger of Allah (Allah's Blessings and Salutations may be on him), while he was at the bed of his death: (Expel the polytheists out of the Arab Peninsula); (narrated by Al Bukhari) and: (If I survive, Allah willing, I'll expel the Jews and the Christians out of the Arab Peninsula); saheeh Aljame' As Sagheer.

9

It is out of date and no longer acceptable to claim that the presence of the crusaders is necessity and only a temporary measures to protect the land of the two Holy Places. Especially when the civil and the military infrastructures of Iraq were savagely destroyed showing the depth of the Zionist-Crusaders hatred to the Muslims and their children, and the rejection of the idea of replacing the crusaders forces by an Islamic force composed of the sons of the country and other Muslim people. moreover the foundations of the claim and the claim it self were demolished and wiped out by the sequence of speeches given by the leaders of the Kuffar in America. The latest of these speeches was the one given by William Perry, the Defense Secretary, after the explosion in Al Khobar saying that: the presence of the American solders there is to protect the interest of the USA. The imprisoned Sheikh Safar Al Hawali, may Allah hasten his release, wrote a book of seventy pages; in it he presented evidence and proof that the presence of the Americans in the Arab Peninsula is a preplanned military occupation. The regime want to deceive the Muslims people in the same manner when the Palestinian fighters, Mujahideen, were deceived causing the loss of Al Aqsa Mosque. In 1304 A.H (1936 CE) the awakened Muslims nation of Palestine started their great struggle, Jihad, against the British occupying forces. Britain was impotent to stop the Mujahideen and their Jihad, but their devil inspired that there is no way to stop the armed struggle in Palestine unless through their agent King Abdul Azeez, who managed to deceives the Mujahideen. King Abdul Azeez carried out his duty to his British masters. He sent his two sons to meet the Mujahideen leaders and to inform them that King Abdul Azeez would guarantee the promises made by the British government in leaving the area and responding positively to the demands of the Mujahideen if the latter stop their Jihad. And so King Abdul Azeez caused the loss of the first Qiblah of the Muslims people. The King joined the crusaders against the Muslims and instead of supporting the Mujahideen in the cause of Allah, to liberate the Al Aqsa Mosque, he disappointed and humiliated them

Today, his son, King Fahd, trying to deceive the Muslims for the second time so as to loose what is left of the sanctities. When the Islamic world resented the arrival of the crusader forces to the land of the two Holy Places, the king told lies to the Ulamah (who issued Fatwas about the arrival of the Americans) and to the gathering of the Islamic leaders at the conference of Rabitah which was held in the Holy City of Makka. The King said that: "the issue is simple, the American and the alliance forces will leave the area in few months". Today it is seven years since their arrival and the regime is not able to move them out of the country. The regime made no confession about its inability and carried on lying to the people claiming that the American will leave. But never never again ; a believer will not be bitten twice from the same hole or snake! Happy is the one who takes note of the sad experience of the others!! Instead of motivating the army, the guards and the security men to oppose the occupiers the regime used these men to protect the invaders, and further deepening the humiliation and the betrayal. (We bemoan this and can only say: "No power and power acquiring except through Allah"). To those little group of men within the army, police and security forces, who have been tricked and pressurized by the regime to attack the Muslims and spill their blood, we would like to remind them of the narration: (I promise war against those who take my friends as their enemy) narrated by Al Bukhari. and his saying (Allah's Blessings and Salutations may be on him) saying of: (In the day of judgement a man comes holding another and complaining being slain by him. Allah, blessed be His Names, asks: Why did you slay him?! The accused replies: I did so that all exaltation may be Yours. Allah, blessed be His Names, says: All exaltation is indeed mine! Another man comes holding a fourth with a similar complaint. Allah, blessed be His Names, asks: Why did you kill him?! The accused replies: I did so that exaltation may be for Mr. X! Allah, blessed be His Names, says: exaltation is mine, not for Mr. X, carry all the slain man's sins (and proceed to the Hell fire)!). In another wording of An Nasa'i: "The accused says: for strengthening the rule or kingdom of Mr. X"

Today your brothers and sons, the sons of the two Holy Places, have started their Jihad in the cause of Allah, to expel the occupying enemy out of the country of the two Holy places. And there is no doubt you would like to carry out this mission too, in order to reestablish the greatness of this Ummah and to liberate its' occupied sanctities. Nevertheless, it must be obvious to you that, due to the imbalance of power between our armed forces and the enemy forces, a suitable means of fighting must be adopted i.e. using fast moving light forces that work under complete secrecy. In other word to initiate a guerrilla warfare, were the sons of the nation, and not the military forces, take part in it. And as you know, it is wise, in the present circumstances, for the armed military forces not to be engaged in a conventional fighting with the forces of the crusader enemy (the exceptions are the bold and the forceful operations carried out by the members of the armed forces individually, that is without the movement of the formal forces in its conventional shape and hence the responses will not be directed, strongly, against the army) unless a big advantage is likely to be achieved; and great losses induced on the enemy side (that would shaken and destroy its foundations and infrastructures) that will help to expel the enemy defeated out of the country. The Mujahideen, your brothers and sons, requesting that you support them in every possible way by supplying them with the necessary information, materials and arms. Security men are especially asked to cover up for the Mujahideen and to assist them as much as possible against the occupying enemy; and to spread rumors, fear and discouragement among the members of the enemy forces. We bring to your attention that the regime, in order to create a friction and feud between the Mujahideen and yourselves, might resort to take a deliberate action against personnel of the security, guards and military forces and blame the Mujahideen for these actions. The regime should not be allowed to have such opportunity. The regime is fully responsible for what had been incurred by the country and the nation; however the occupying American enemy is the principle and the main cause of the situation . Therefore efforts should be concentrated on destroying, fighting and killing the enemy until, by the Grace of Allah, it is completely defeated. The time will come by the Permission of Allah when you'll perform your decisive role so that the word of Allah will be supreme and the word of the infidels (Kaferoon) will be the inferior. You will hit with iron fist against the aggressors. You'll reestablish the normal course and give the people their rights and carry out your truly Islamic duty. Allah willing, I'll have a separate talk about these issues.

My Muslim Brothers (particularly those of the Arab Peninsula):

The money you pay to buy American goods will be transformed into bullets and used against our brothers in Palestine and tomorrow (future) against our sons in the land of the two

Holy places. By buying these goods we are strengthening their economy while our dispossession and poverty increases.

Muslims Brothers of land of the two Holy Places:

It is incredible that our country is the world largest buyer of arms from the USA and the area biggest commercial partners of the Americans who are assisting their Zionist brothers in occupying Palestine and in evicting and killing the Muslims there, by providing arms, men and financial supports. To deny these occupiers from the enormous revenues of their trading with our country is a very important help for our Jihad against them. To express our anger and hate to them is a very important moral gesture. By doing so we would have taken part in (the process of) cleansing our sanctities from the crusaders and the Zionists and forcing them, by the Permission of Allah, to leave disappointed and defeated.

We expect the woman of the land of the two Holy Places and other countries to carry out their role in boycotting the American goods. If economical boycotting is intertwined with the military operations of the Mujahideen, then defeating the enemy will be even nearer, by the Permission of Allah. However if Muslims don't cooperate and support their Mujahideen brothers then , in effect, they are supplying the army of the enemy with financial help and extending the war and increasing the suffering of the Muslims.

The security and the intelligence services of the entire world can not force a single citizen to buy the goods of his/her enemy. Economical boycotting of the American goods is a very effective weapon of hitting and weakening the enemy, and it is not under the control of the security forces of the regime. Before closing my talk, I have a very important message to the youths of Islam, men of the brilliant future of the Ummah of Muhammad (ALLAH'S BLESSING AND SALUTATIONS ON HIM). Our talk with the youths about their duty in this difficult period in the history of our Ummah. A period in which the youths and no one else came forward to carry out the variable and different duties. While some of the well known individuals had hesitated in their duty of defending Islam and saving themselves and their wealth from the injustice, aggression and terror exercised by the government the youths (may Allah protect them) were forthcoming and raised the banner of Jihad against the American-Zionist alliance occupying the sanctities of Islam. Others who have been tricked into loving this materialistic world, and those who have been terrorized by the government choose to give legitimacy to the greatest betrayal , the occupation of the land of the two Holy Places (We bemoan this and can only say: "No power and power acquiring except through Allah"). We are not surprised from the action of our youths. The youths were the companions of Muhammad (Allah's Blessings and Salutations may be on him), and was it not the youths themselves who killed Aba Jahl, the Pharaoh of this Ummah?. Our youths are the best descendent of the best ancestors.

Abdul Rahman Ibn Awf may Allah be pleased with him said: (I was at Badr where I noticed two youths one to my right and the other to my left. One of them asked me quietly (so not to be heard by the other): O uncle, point out Aba Jahl to me. What do you want him for, said Abdul Rahman? The boy answered: I have been informed that he Aba Jahl abused the Messenger of Allah (SAW), I swear by Allah, who have my soul in His hand, that if I see Aba Jahl I'll not let my shadow departs his shadow till one of us is dead. I was astonished, said Abdul Rahman; then the other youth said the same thing as the first one. Subsequently I saw Aba Jahl among the people; I said to the boys do you see? This is the man you are asking me about. The two youths hit Aba Jahl with their swords till he was dead. Allah is the greatest, Praise be to Him: Two youths of young age but with great perseverance, enthusiasm, courage and pride for the religion of Allah's, each one of them asking about the most important act of killing that should be induced on the enemy. That is the killing of the pharaoh of this Ummah Aba Jahl, the leader of the unbelievers (Mushrikeen) at the battle of Badr. The role of Abdul Rahman Ibn Awf, may Allah be pleased with him, was to direct the two youths toward Aba Jahl. That was the perseverance and the enthusiasm of the youths of that time and that was the perseverance and the enthusiasm of their fathers. It is this role that is now required from the people who have the expertise and knowledge in fighting the enemy. They should guide their brothers and sons in this matter; once that has been done, then our youths will repeat what their forefathers had said before: "I swear by Allah if I see him I'll not let my shadow to departs from his shadow till one of us is dead".

And the story of Abdur Rahman Ibn Awf about Ummayyah Ibn Khalaf shows the extent of Bilal's (may Allah be pleased with him) persistence in killing the head of the Kufr: "the head of Kufr is Ummayyah Ibn Khalaf.... I shall live not if he survives" said Bilal.
Few days ago the news agencies had reported that the Defense Secretary of the Crusading Americans had said that "the explosion at Riyadh and Al Khobar had taught him one lesson: that is not to withdraw when attacked by coward terrorists".
We say to the Defense Secretary that his talk can induce a grieving mother to laughter! and shows the fears that had enshrined you all. Where was this false courage of yours when the explosion in Beirut took place on 1983 CE (1403 A.H). You were turned into scattered pits and pieces at that time; 241 mainly marines solders were killed. And where was this courage of yours when two explosions made you to leave Aden in less than twenty four hours!

But your most disgraceful case was in Somalia; wherefore vigorous propaganda about the power of the USA and its post cold war leadership of the new world order you moved tens of thousands of international force, including twenty eight thousands American solders into Somalia. However, when tens of your solders were killed in minor battles and one American Pilot was dragged in the streets of Mogadishu you left the area carrying disappointment, humiliation, defeat and your dead with you. Clinton appeared in front of the whole world threatening and promising revenge , but these threats were merely a preparation for withdrawal. You have been disgraced by Allah and you withdrew; the extent of your impotence and weaknesses became very clear. It was a pleasure for the "heart" of every Muslim and a remedy to the "chests" of believing nations to see you defeated in the three Islamic cities of Beirut , Aden and Mogadishu.

I say to Secretary of Defense: The sons of the land of the two Holy Places had come out to fight against the Russian in Afghanistan, the Serb in Bosnia Herzegovina and today they are fighting in Chechnya and by the Permission of Allah they have been made victorious over your partner, the Russians. By the command of Allah, they are also fighting in Tajakistan. 1 I'll not let my shadow departs his shadow till one of us is dead. I was astonished, said Abdul Rahman; then the other youth said the same thing as the first one. Subsequently I saw Aba Jahl among the people; I said to the boys do you see? this is the man you are asking me about. The two youths hit Aba Jahl with their swords till he was dead. Allah is the greatest, Praise be to Him: Two youths of young age but with great perseverance, enthusiasm, courage and pride for the religion of Allah's, each one of them asking about the most important act of killing that should be induced on the enemy. That is the killing of the pharaoh of this Ummah Aba Jahl, the leader of the unbelievers (Mushrikeen) at the battle of Badr. The role of Abdul Rahman Ibn Awf , may Allah be pleased with him, was to direct the two youths toward Aba Jahl. That was the perseverance and the enthusiasm of the youths of that time and that was the perseverance and the enthusiasm of their fathers. It is this role that is now required from the people who have the expertise and knowledge in fighting the enemy. They should guide their brothers and sons in this matter; once that has been done, then our youths will repeat what their forefathers had said before: "I swear by Allah if I see him I'll not let my shadow to departs from his shadow till one of us is dead".

And the story of Abdur Rahman Ibn Awf about Ummayyah Ibn Khalaf shows the extent of Bilal's (may Allah be pleased with him) persistence in killing the head of the Kufr: "the head of Kufr is Ummayyah Ibn Khalaf.... I shall live not if he survives" said Bilal.

Few days ago the news agencies had reported that the Defense Secretary of the Crusading Americans had said that "the explosion at Riyadh and Al Khobar had taught him one lesson: that is not to withdraw when attacked by coward terrorists".

We say to the Defense Secretary that his talk can induce a grieving mother to laughter! and shows the fears that had enshrined you all. Where was this false courage of yours when the explosion in Beirut took place on 1983 CE (1403 A.H). You were turned into scattered pits and pieces at that time; 241 mainly marines solders were killed. And where was this courage of yours when two explosions made you to leave Aden in less than twenty four hours!

But your most disgraceful case was in Somalia; wherefore vigorous propaganda about the power of the USA and its post cold war leadership of the new world order you moved tens of thousands of international force, including twenty eight thousands American solders into Somalia. However, when tens of your solders were killed in minor battles and one American Pilot was dragged in the streets of Mogadishu you left the area carrying disappointment, humiliation, defeat and your dead with you. Clinton appeared in front of the whole world threatening and promising revenge , but these threats were merely a preparation for withdrawal. You have been disgraced by Allah and you withdrew; the extent of your impotence and weaknesses became very clear. It was a pleasure for the "heart" of every Muslim and a remedy to the "chests" of believing nations to see you defeated in the three Islamic cities of Beirut , Aden and Mogadishu.

I say to Secretary of Defense: The sons of the land of the two Holy Places had come out to fight against the Russian in Afghanistan, the Serb in Bosnia Herzegovina and today they are fighting in Chechnya and by the Permission of Allah they have been made victorious over your partner, the Russians. By the command of Allah, they are also fighting in Tajikistan.

I say: Since the sons of the land of the two Holy Places feel and strongly believe that fighting (Jihad) against the Kuffar in every part of the world, is absolutely essential; then they would be even more enthusiastic, more powerful and larger in number upon fighting on their own land the place of their births defending the greatest of their sanctities, the noble Ka'ba (the Qiblah of all Muslims). They know that the Muslims of the world will assist and help them to victory. To liberate their sanctities is the greatest of issues concerning all Muslims; It is the duty of every Muslims in this world. I say to you William (Defense Secretary) that: These youths love death as you loves life. They inherit dignity, pride, courage, generosity, truthfulness and sacrifice from father to father. They are most delivering and steadfast at war. They inherit these values from their ancestors (even from the time of the Jaheliyyah, before Islam). These values were approved and completed by the arriving Islam as stated by the messenger of Allah (Allah's Blessings and Salutations may be on him): "I have been send to perfecting the good values". (Saheeh Al Jame' As Sagheer). When the pagan King Amroo Ibn Hind tried to humiliate the pagan Amroo Ibn Kulthoom, the latter cut the head of the King with his sword rejecting aggression, humiliation and indignation.

If the king oppresses the people excessively, we reject to submit to humiliation.

By which legitimacy (or command) O Amroo bin Hind you want us to be degraded?!

By which legitimacy (or command) O Amroo bin Hind you listen to our foes and disrespect us?!

Our toughness has, O Amroo, tired the enemies before you, never giving in! Our youths believe in paradise after death. They believe that taking part in fighting will not bring their day nearer; and staying behind will not postpone their day either. Exalted be to Allah who said: {And a soul will not die but with the permission of Allah, the term is fixed} (Aal Imraan; 3:145). Our youths believe in the saying of the messenger of Allah (Allah's Blessings and Salutations may be on him): "O boy, I teach a few words; guard (guard the cause of, keep the commandments of) Allah, then He guards you, guard (the cause of) Allah, then He will be with you; if you ask (for your need) ask Allah, if you seek assistance, seek Allah's; and know definitely that if the Whole World gathered to (bestow) profit on you they will not profit you except with what was determined for you by Allah, and if they gathered to harm you they will not harm you except with what has been determined for you by Allah; Pen lifted, papers dried, it is fixed nothing in these truths can be changed" Saheeh Al Jame' As Sagheer.

Our youths took note of the meaning of the poetic verse:

"if death is a predetermined must, then it is a shame to die cowardly"

and the other poet saying:

"who do not die by the sword will die by other reason; many causes are there but one death".

These youths believe in what has been told by Allah and His messenger (Allah's Blessings and Salutations may be on him) about the greatness of the reward for the Mujahideen and Martyrs; Allah, the most exalted said: {and so far those who are slain in the way of Allah, He will by no means allow their deeds to perish. He will guide them and improve their condition. and cause them to enter the garden paradise which He has made known to them}. (Muhammad;47:46). Allah the Exalted also said: {and do not speak of those who are slain in Allah's way as dead; nay they are alive, but you do not perceive} (Bagarah; 2:154). His messenger (Allah's Blessings and Salutations may be on him) said: "for those who strive in His cause Allah prepared hundred degrees (levels) in paradise; in-between two degrees as the in-between heaven and earth". Saheeh Al Jame' As Sagheer. He (Allah's Blessings and Salutations may be on him) also said: "the best of the martyrs are those who do NOT turn their faces away from the battle till they are killed. They are in the high level of Jannah (paradise). Their Lord laughs to them (in pleasure) and when your Lord laughs to a slave of His, He will not hold him to an account". narrated by Ahmad with correct and trustworthy reference. And : "a martyr will not feel the pain of death except like how you feel when you are pinched". Saheeh Al Jame' As Sagheer. He also said : "a martyr privileges are guaranteed by Allah; forgiveness with the first gush of his blood, he will be shown his seat in paradise, he will be decorated with the jewels of belief (Imaan), married off to the beautiful ones, protected from the test in the grave, assured security in the day of judgement, crowned with the crown of dignity, a ruby of which is better than this whole world (Duniah) and its' entire content, wedded to seventy two of the pure Houries (beautiful ones of Paradise) and his intercession on the behalf of seventy of his relatives will be accepted". narrated by Ahmad and At Tirmithi (with the correct and trustworthy reference).

Those youths know that their rewards in fighting you, the USA, is double than their rewards in fighting some one else not from the people of the book. They have no intention except to enter paradise by killing you. An infidel, and enemy of God like you, cannot be in the same hell with his righteous executioner. Our youths chanting and reciting the word of Allah, the most exalted:

{fight them; Allah will punish them by your hands and bring them to disgrace, and assist you against them and heal the heart of a believing people} (At Taubah; 9:14) and the words of the prophet (ALLAH'S BLESSING AND SALUTATIONS ON HIM): "I swear by Him, who has my soul in His hand, that no man get killed fighting them today, patiently attacking and not retreating ,surely Allah will let him into paradise". And his (Allah's Blessings and Salutations may be on him) saying to them: "get up to a paradise as wide as heaven and earth".

The youths also reciting the All Mighty words of: {so when you meet in battle those who disbelieve, then smite the necks........} (Muhammad; 47:19).

Those youths will not ask you (William Perry) for explanations, they will tell you singing there is nothing between us need to be explained, there is only killing and neck smiting.

And they will say to you what their grand father, Haroon Ar Rasheed, Ameerul Mu'meneen, replied to your grandfather, Nagfoor, the Byzantine emperor, when he threatened the Muslims: "from Haroon Ar Rasheed, Ameerul Mu'meneen, to Nagfoor, the dog of the Romans; the answer is what you will see not what you hear". Haroon El Rasheed led the armies of Islam to the battle and handed Nagfoor a devastating defeat.

The youths you called cowards are competing among themselves for fighting and killing you. reciting what one of them said:

The crusader army became dust when we detonated al Khobar With courageous youth of Islam fearing no danger.

If (they are) threatened: The tyrants will kill you, they reply my death is a victory I did not betrayed that king, he did betray our Qiblah

And he permitted in the holy country the most filthy sort of humans. I have made an oath by Allah, the Great, to fight who ever rejected the faith

For more than a decade, they carried arms on their shoulders in Afghanistan and they have made vows to Allah that as long as they are alive, they will continue to carry arms against you until you are Allah willing expelled, defeated and humiliated, they will carry on as long as they live saying:

O William, tomorrow you will know which young man is confronting your misguided brethren!

A youth fighting in smile, returning with the spear colored red.

May Allah keep me close to knights, humans in peace, demons in war.

Lions in Jungle but their teeth are spears and Indian swords.

The horses witness that I push them hard forwarded in the fire of battle.

The dust of the battle bears witnesses for me, so also the fighting itself, the pens and the books!

So to abuse the grandsons of the companions, may Allah be pleased with them, by calling them cowards and challenging them by refusing to leave the land of the two Holy Places shows the insanity and the imbalance you are suffering from. Its appropriate `remedy ,however, is in the hands of the youths of Islam, as the poet said:

I am willing to sacrifice self and wealth for knights who never disappointed me Knights who are never fed up or deterred by death, even if the mill of war turns

17

Appendix 1 A

In the heat of battle they do not care, and cure the insanity of the enemy by their 'insane' courage. Terrorizing you, while you are carrying arms on our land, is a legitimate and morally demanded duty. It is a legitimate right well known to all humans and other creatures. Your example and our example is like a snake which entered into a house of a man and got killed by him. The coward is the one who lets you walk, while carrying arms, freely on his land and provides you with peace and security.

Those youths are different from your soldiers. Your problem will be how to convince your troops to fight, while our problem will be how to restrain our youths to wait for their turn in fighting and in operations. These youths are commendation and praiseworthy.

They stood up tall to defend the religion; at the time when the government misled the prominent scholars and tricked them into issuing Fatwas (that have no basis neither in the book of Allah, nor in the Sunnah of His prophet (Allah's Blessings and Salutations may be on him)) of opening the land of the two Holy Places for the Christians armies and handing the Al Aqsa Mosque to the Zionists.

Twisting the meanings of the holy text will not change this fact at all. They deserve the praise of the poet:

I rejected all the critics, who chose the wrong way

I rejected those who enjoy fireplaces in clubs discussing eternally

I rejected those, who inspite being lost, think they are at the goal

I respect those who carried on not asking or bothering about the difficulties

Never letting up from their goals, inspite all hardships of the road

Whose blood is the oil for the flame guiding in the darkness of confusion

I feel still the pain of (the loss) Al Quds in my internal organs.

That loss is like a burning fire in my intestines

I did not betray my covenant with God, when even states did betray it!

As their grand father Assim Bin Thabit said rejecting a surrender offer of the pagans:

What for an excuse I had to surrender, while I am still able, having arrows and my bow having a tough string?!

Death is truth and ultimate destiny, and life will end any way.

18

If I do not fight you, then my mother must be insane!

The youths hold you responsible for all of the killings and evictions of the Muslims and the violation of the sanctities, carried out by your Zionist brothers in Lebanon; you openly supplied them with arms and finance. More than 600,000 Iraqi children have died due to lack of food and medicine and as a result of the unjustifiable aggression (sanction) imposed on Iraq and its nation.

The children of Iraq are our children. You, the USA, together with the Saudi regime are responsible for the shedding of the blood of these innocent children. Due to all of that, what ever treaty you have with our country is now null and void.

The treaty of Hudaybiyyah was cancelled by the messenger of Allah (Allah's Blessings and Salutations may be on him) once Quraysh had assisted Bani Bakr against Khusa'ah , the allies of the prophet (Allah's Blessings and Salutations may be on him). The prophet (Allah's Blessings and Salutations may be on him) fought Quraysh and concurred Makka. He (Allah's Blessings and Salutations may be on him) considered the treaty with Bani Qainuqa' void because one of their Jews publicly hurt one Muslim woman, one single woman, at the market. Let alone then, the killing you caused to hundred of thousands Muslims and occupying their sanctities. It is now clear that those who claim that the blood of the American solders (the enemy occupying the land of the Muslims) should be protected are merely repeating what is imposed on them by the regime; fearing the aggression and interested in saving themselves. It is a duty now on every tribe in the Arab Peninsula to fight, Jihad, in the cause of Allah and to cleanse the land from those occupiers. Allah knows that there blood is permitted (to be spilled) and their wealth is a booty; their wealth is a booty to those who kill them. The most Exalted said in the verse of As Sayef, The Sword: {so when the sacred months have passed away, then slay the idolaters where ever you find them, and take them captives and besiege them and lie in wait for them in every ambush} (At Tauba; 9:5). Our youths knew that the humiliation suffered by the Muslims as a result of the occupation of their sanctities can not be kicked and removed except by explosions and Jihad. As the poet said:

The walls of oppression and humiliation cannot be demolished except in a rain of bullets
The freeman does not surrender leadership to infidels and sinners

Without shedding blood no degradation and branding can be removed from the forehead
I remind the youths of the Islamic world, who fought in Afghanistan and Bosnia Herzegovina with their wealth, pens, tongues and themselves that the battle had not finished yet. I remind them about the talk between Jibreel (Gabriel) and the messenger of Allah (Allah's Blessings and Salutations may be on both of them) after the battle of Ahzab when the messenger of Allah (Allah's Blessings and Salutations may be on him) returned to Medina and before putting his sword aside; when Jibreel (Allah's Blessings and Salutations may be on him) descend saying: "are you putting your sword aside? by Allah the angels haven't dropped their arms yet; march with your companions to Bani Quraydah, I am (going) ahead of you to throw fears in their hearts

19

and to shake their fortresses on them". Jibreel marched with the angels (Allah's Blessings and Salutations may be on them all), followed by the messenger of Allah (Allah's Blessings and Salutations may be on him) marching with the immigrants, Muhajeroon, and supporters, Ansar. (narrated by Al Bukhary).

These youths know that: if one is not to be killed one will die (any way) and the most honorable death is to be killed in the way of Allah. They are even more determined after the martyrdom of the four heroes who bombed the Americans in Riyadh. Those youths who raised high the head of the Ummah and humiliated the Americans the occupier by their operation in Riyadh. They remember the poetry of Ja'far, the second commander in the battle of Mu'tah, in which three thousand Muslims faced over a hundred thousand Romans:

How good is the Paradise and its nearness, good with cool drink

But the Romans are promised punishment (in Hell), if I meet them

I will fight them.

And the poetry of Abdullah Bin Rawaha, the third commander in the battle of Mu'tah, after the martyrdom of Ja'far, when he felt some hesitation:

O my soul if you do not get killed, you are going to die, anyway.

This is death pool in front of you!

You are getting what you have wished for (martyrdom) before, and you follow the example of the two previous commanders you are rightly guided!

As for our daughters, wives, sisters and mothers they should take prime example from the prophet (Allah's Blessings and Salutations may be on him) pious female companions, may Allah be pleased with them; they should adopt the life style (Seerah) of the female companions of courage, sacrifice and generosity in the cause of the supremacy of Allah's religion. They should remember the courage and the personality of Fatima, daughter of Khatab, when she accepted Islam and stood up in front of her brother, Omar Ibn Al Khatab and challenged him (before he became a Muslim) saying: "O Omar , what will you do if the truth is not in your religion?!" And to remember the stand of Asma', daughter of Abu Bakr, on the day of Hijra, when she attended the Messenger and his companion in the cave and split her belt in two pieces for them. And to remember the stand of Naseeba Bent Ka'b striving to defend the messenger of Allah (Allah's Blessings and Salutations may be on him) on the day of Uhud, in which she suffered twelve injuries, one of which was so deep leaving a deep lifelong scar! They should remember the generosity of the early woman of Islam who raised finance for the Muslims army by selling their jewelry. Our women had set a tremendous example of generosity in the cause of Allah; they motivated and encouraged their sons, brothers and husbands to fight in the cause of Allah in Afghanistan, Bosnia Herzegovina, Chechnya and in other countries. We ask Allah to accept from them these deeds, and may He help their fathers, brothers, husbands and sons. May Allah strengthen the belief Imaan of our women in the way of generosity and sacrifice for the supremacy of the word of Allah. Our women weep not, except over men who fight in the cause of Allah; our women instigate their brothers to fight in the cause of Allah.

Our women bemoan only fighters in the cause of Allah, as said:

Do not moan on any one except a lion in the woods, courageous in the burning wars

Let me die dignified in wars, honorable death is better than my current life

Our women encourage to Jihad saying:

Prepare yourself like a struggler, the matter is bigger than words!

Are you going to leave us else for the wolves of Kufr eating our wings?!

The wolves of Kufr are mobilizing all evil persons from every where!

Where are the freemen defending free women by the arms?!

Death is better than life in humiliation! Some scandals and shames will never be otherwise eradicated.

My Muslim Brothers of The World:

Your brothers in Palestine and in the land of the two Holy Places are calling upon your help and asking you to take part in fighting against the enemy your enemy and their enemy the Americans and the Israelis. they are asking you to do whatever you can, with one own means and ability, to expel the enemy, humiliated and defeated, out of the sanctities of Islam. Exalted be to Allah said in His book: { and if they ask your support, because they are oppressed in their faith, then support them!} (Anfaal; 8:72)

O you horses (soldiers) of Allah ride and march on. This is the time of hardship so be tough. And know that your gathering and cooperation in order to liberate the sanctities of Islam is the right step toward unifying the word of the Ummah under the banner of "No God but Allah").

From our place we raise our palms humbly to Allah asking Him to bestow on us His guide in every aspects of this issue.

Our Lord, we ask you to secure the release of the truthful scholars, Ulama, of Islam and pious youths of the Ummah from their imprisonment. O Allah, strengthen them and help their families.

Our Lord, the people of the cross had come with their horses (soldiers)and occupied the land of the two Holy places. And the Zionist Jews fiddling as they wish with the Al Aqsa Mosque, the route of the ascendance of the messenger of Allah (ALLAH'S BLESSING AND SALUTATIONS ON HIM). Our Lord, shatter their gathering, divide them among themselves, shaken the earth under their feet and give us control over them; Our Lord, we take refuge in you from their deeds and take you as a shield between us and them

Our Lord, show us a black day in them!

Our Lord, show us the wonderment of your ability in them!

Our Lord , You are the Revealer of the book, Director of the clouds,
You defeated the allies (Ahzab); defeat them and make us victorious over them.

Our Lord, You are the one who help us and You are the one who assist us, with Your Power we move and by Your Power we fight. On You we rely and You are our cause. Our Lord, those youths got together to make Your religion victorious and raise Your banner. Our Lord, send them Your help and strengthen their hearts.

Our Lord, make the youths of Islam steadfast and descend patience on them and guide their shots!

Our Lord, unify the Muslims and bestow love among their hearts!

Our Lord, pour down upon us patience, and make our steps firm and assist us against the unbelieving people!

Our Lord, do not lay on us a burden as Thou didst lay on those before us; Our Lord, do not impose upon us that which we have no strength to bear; and pardon us and grant us protection and have mercy on us, Thou art our patron, so help us against the unbelieving people.

Our Lord, guide this Ummah, and make the right conditions (by which) the people of your obedience will be in dignity and the people of disobedience in humiliation, and by which the good deeds are enjoined and the bad deeds are forebode.

Our Lord, bless Muhammad, Your slave and messenger, his family and descendants, and companions and salute him with a (becoming) salutation.
And our last supplication is: All praise is due to Allah .

Usamah bin Muhammad bin Laden
Friday, 9/4/1417 A.H (23/8/1996 CE) Hindukush Mountains, Khurasan, Afghanistan.

Jihad Against Jews and Crusaders

World Islamic Front Statement*

February 23, 1998

Shaykh Usamah Bin-Muhammad Bin-Ladin
Ayman al-Zawahiri, amir of the Jihad Group in Egypt
Abu-Yasir Rifa'i Ahmad Taha, Egyptian Islamic Group
Shaykh Mir Hamzah, secretary of the Jamiat-ul-Ulema-e-Pakistan
Fazlul Rahman, amir of the Jihad Movement in Bangladesh

Praise be to God, who revealed the Book, controls the clouds, defeats factionalism, and says in His Book: "But when the forbidden months are past, then fight and slay the pagans wherever ye find them, seize them, beleaguer them, and lie in wait for them in every stratagem (of war)"; and peace be upon our Prophet, Muhammad Bin-'Abdallah, who said: I have been sent with the sword between my hands to ensure that no one but God is worshipped, God who put my livelihood under the shadow of my spear and who inflicts humiliation and scorn on those who disobey my orders.

The Arabian Peninsula has never -- since God made it flat, created its desert, and encircled it with seas -- been stormed by any forces like the crusader armies spreading in it like locusts, eating its riches and wiping out its plantations. All this is happening at a time in which nations are attacking Muslims like people fighting over a plate of food. In the light of the grave situation and the lack of support, we and you are obliged to discuss current events, and we should all agree on how to settle the matter.

No one argues today about three facts that are known to everyone; we will list them, in order to remind everyone:

First, for over seven years the United States has been occupying the lands of Islam in the holiest of places, the Arabian Peninsula, plundering its riches, dictating to its rulers, humiliating its people, terrorizing its neighbors, and turning its bases in the Peninsula into a spearhead through which to fight the neighboring Muslim peoples.

If some people have in the past argued about the fact of the occupation, all the people of the Peninsula have now acknowledged it. The best proof of this is the Americans' continuing aggression against the Iraqi people using the Peninsula as a staging post, even though all its rulers are against their territories being used to that end, but they are helpless.

---

* Source: Federation of American Scientists (FAS)

http://www.fas.org/irp/world/para/docs/980223-fatwa.htm

Second, despite the great devastation inflicted on the Iraqi people by the crusader-Zionist alliance, and despite the huge number of those killed, which has exceeded 1 million... despite all this, the Americans are once against trying to repeat the horrific massacres, as though they are not content with the protracted blockade imposed after the ferocious war or the fragmentation and devastation.

So here they come to annihilate what is left of this people and to humiliate their Muslim neighbors.

Third, if the Americans' aims behind these wars are religious and economic, the aim is also to serve the Jews' petty state and divert attention from its occupation of Jerusalem and murder of Muslims there. The best proof of this is their eagerness to destroy Iraq, the strongest neighboring Arab state, and their endeavor to fragment all the states of the region such as Iraq, Saudi Arabia, Egypt, and Sudan into paper statelets and through their disunion and weakness to guarantee Israel's survival and the continuation of the brutal crusade occupation of the Peninsula.

All these crimes and sins committed by the Americans are a clear declaration of war on God, his messenger, and Muslims. And ulema have throughout Islamic history unanimously agreed that the jihad is an individual duty if the enemy destroys the Muslim countries. This was revealed by Imam Bin-Qadamah in "Al- Mughni," Imam al-Kisa'i in "Al-Bada'i," al-Qurtubi in his interpretation, and the shaykh of al-Islam in his books, where he said: "As for the fighting to repulse [an enemy], it is aimed at defending sanctity and religion, and it is a duty as agreed [by the ulema]. Nothing is more sacred than belief except repulsing an enemy who is attacking religion and life."

On that basis, and in compliance with God's order, we issue the following fatwa to all Muslims:

The ruling to kill the Americans and their allies -- civilians and military -- is an individual duty for every Muslim who can do it in any country in which it is possible to do it, in order to liberate the al-Aqsa Mosque and the holy mosque [Mecca] from their grip, and in order for their armies to move out of all the lands of Islam, defeated and unable to threaten any Muslim. This is in accordance with the words of Almighty God, "and fight the pagans all together as they fight you all together," and "fight them until there is no more tumult or oppression, and there prevail justice and faith in God."

This is in addition to the words of Almighty God: "And why should ye not fight in the cause of God and of those who, being weak, are ill-treated (and oppressed)? -- women and children, whose cry is: 'Our Lord, rescue us from this town, whose people are oppressors; and raise for us from thee one who will help!'"

We -- with God's help -- call on every Muslim who believes in God and wishes to be rewarded to comply with God's order to kill the Americans and plunder their money wherever and whenever they find it. We also call on Muslim ulema, leaders, youths, and

2

people. An injustice that had affected every section and group of the people; the civilians, military and security men, government officials and merchants, the young and the old people as well as schools and university students. Hundred of thousands of the unemployed graduates, who became the widest section of the society, were also affected.

Injustice had affected the people of the industry and agriculture. It affected the people of the rural and urban areas. And almost every body complain about something. The situation at the land of the two Holy places became like a huge volcano at the verge of eruption that would destroy the Kufr and the corruption and its' sources. The explosion at Riyadh and Al Khobar is a warning of this volcanic eruption emerging as a result of the sever oppression, suffering, excessive iniquity, humiliation and poverty.

People are fully concerned about their every day livings; every body talks about the deterioration of the economy, inflation, ever increasing debts and jails full of prisoners. Government employees with limited income talk about debts of ten thousands and hundred thousands of Saudi Riyals. They complain that the value of the Riyal is greatly and continuously deteriorating among most of the main currencies. Great merchants and contractors speak about hundreds and thousands of million Riyals owed to them by the government. More than three hundred forty billions of Riyal owed by the government to the people in addition to the daily accumulated interest, let alone the foreign debt. People wonder whether we are the largest oil exporting country?! They even believe that this situation is a curse put on them by Allah for not objecting to the oppressive and illegitimate behavior and measures of the ruling regime:

Ignoring the divine Shari'ah law; depriving people of their legitimate rights; allowing the American to occupy the land of the two Holy Places; imprisonment, unjustly, of the sincere scholars. The honorable Ulamah and scholars as well as merchants, economists and eminent people of the country were all alerted by this disastrous situation.

Quick efforts were made by each group to contain and to correct the situation. All agreed that the country is heading toward a great catastrophe, the depth of which is not known except by Allah. One big merchant commented: `` the king is leading the state into `sixty-six' folded disaster", (We bemoan this and can only say: "No power and power acquiring except through Allah"). Numerous princes share with the people their feelings, privately expressing their concerns and objecting to the corruption, repression and the intimidation taking place in the country. But the competition between influential princes for personal gains and interest had destroyed the country. Through its course of actions the regime has torn off its legitimacy:

(1) Suspension of the Islamic Shari'ah law and exchanging it with man made civil law. The regime entered into a bloody confrontation with the truthful Ulamah and the righteous youths (we sanctify nobody; Allah sanctify Whom He pleaseth).

(2) The inability of the regime to protect the country, and allowing the enemy of the Ummah the American crusader forces to occupy the land for the longest of years. The crusader forces became the main cause of our disastrous condition, particularly in the economical aspect of it due

Interviews with Usama bin Laden

Mujahid Usamah Bin Ladin
Talks Exclusively to "NIDA'UL ISLAM" About

The New Powder Keg in The Middle East*

Q: What is the policy that should be adopted by the Islamic movement towards the scholars who defend -intentionally or unintentionally- the likes of the Saud regime?

It is not a concealed fact that the police states in the Arab world rely on some foundations in order to protect themselves.. Amongst these organisations is the security organisation as they spend generously on it, and its foremost mission is to spy on its own people in order to protect the person of the ruler, even if this was at the expense of the rights of the people and their security, as also the military sector, which is prepared to strike the people if they wish to reject the suppression and to remove oppression and establish truth.

The media sector is in the same category as it strives to beatify the persons of the leaders, to drowse the community, and to fulfil the plans of the enemies through keeping the people occupied with the minor matters, and to stir their emotions and desires until corruption becomes widespread amongst the believers.

There is also another organisation which takes priority with the leaders in the Arab world, and is used to take the people astray, and to open the door wide for the security factions to fulfil their aforementioned objectives. This is the organisation of the scholars of the authorities, as the role of this organisation is the most dangerous of roles in the entirety of the Arabic countries.

History is the best witness to this.

At the same time that some of the leaders are engaging in the major Kufr, which takes them out of the fold of Islam in broad daylight and in front of all the people, you would find a Fatwa from their religious organisation. In particular, the role of the religious organisation in the country of the two sacred mosques is of the most ominous of roles, this is overlooking whether it fulfilled this role intentionally or unintentionally, the harm which eventuated from their efforts is no different from the role of the most ardent enemies of the nation.

The regime in the land of the two sacred mosques has given a very high priority to this organisation, and has been able to enlarge its position in the estimation of the people until it made of it an idol to be worshipped aside from God amongst some of the common people, and without the will of the members of this organisation.

---

* This article was published in the 15th issue of the *Nida'ul Islam (The Call of Islam) Magazine* (Sydney, Australia), October-November 1996. Printed with Permission
http://www.islam.org.au/articles/15/LADIN.htm

1

However, there continues to be in the land of the two sacred mosques - with gratitude to Allah - a good number of honest scholars and students who work according to their teachings, and those who have taken visible and daring stances against the Kufr activities which the regime is working.

The regime has strived to keep these scholars in the shadows and then removed them, one way or another, from being effective elements in the lives of the people in the community. At the forefront of these scholars was the Sheikh Abdullah Bin Hamid - May Allah bless his soul - who was the Mufti in the Arabian peninsula, and who headed the supreme council of judges. However, the regime constrained him and tightened their grip on him until he offered his resignation.. He has many famous writings in response to the unacceptable laws which the government had introduced instead of the Law of Allah, one of these is a treatise dealing with the law of work and workers which deals with many of the introduced laws which contradict the law of Allah (s.w.t.).

At the same time, they promoted some of the scholars who were far below Sheikh Ibn Hamid - may Allah bless his soul - those who have been known to be weak and soft, so they put them forward in a cunning plan which began more than twenty years ago.. During the preceding two decades, the regime enlarged the role of Bin Baz (Grand Mufti) because of what it knows of his weakness and flexibility and the ease of influencing him with the various means which the interior ministry practices through providing him with false information. So, a generation of youth were raised believing that the most pious and knowledgeable of people is Bin Baz as a result of the media promotion through a well studied policy which had been progressed over twenty years.
After this, the government began to strike with the cane of Bin Baz, every corrective programme which the honest scholars put forward, further, it extracted a Fatwa to hand over Palestine to the Jews, and before this, to permit entry into the country of the two sacred mosques to the modern day crusaders under the rule of necessity, then it relied on a letter from him to the minister for internal affairs and placed the honest scholars in the gaols.

The confidence of the people and the youth in Bin Baz was therefore shaken, however the price was very high, whilst the confidence of the people in the working scholars, particularly those in the prisons had been increased.

The policy of the Organisation for Advice and Rectification towards these scholars is the continuation of providing advise to them openly and secretly (as there is no person above the law, and we are not immune) and particularly in the matters where they gave public rulings, and to bring the rulings of the scholars who respond to their rulings, in order to bring awareness to the people as to the correct ruling with respect to these matters, and not to forestall the rectification programme so that the scholars are made aware, as the pressure which is applied against them is very great.

Also the promotion of the honest scholars and their mention with what they deserve in front of the people so that the confidence of the people would greatly shift in support to them.

Q: How do you evaluate the Saud regime's foreign policy towards the Muslim world in the past years?

The external policy of the Saud regime towards Islamic issues is a policy which is tied to the British outlook from the establishment of Saudi Arabia until 1364 ah (1945 ac), then it became attached to the American outlook after America gained prominence as a major power in the world after the Second World War.

It is well known that the policies of these two countries bear the greatest enmity towards the Islamic world.

To be taken out of this category is the final phase of the rule of King Faisal, as there was a clear interest with the Muslim issues, in particular al Quds and Palestine.
However, the regime does not cease to cry in the open over the matters effecting the Muslims without making any serious effort to serve the interests of the Muslim community apart from small efforts in order to confuse people and throw some dust into their eyes.

Q: The confrontation between the Islamic movement and the apostate Saud regime recorded a historical turning point following the latest attacks against the American occupiers targets. How did these attacks reflect on the internal front, and how did they affect the Saudi-American relations?

There were important effects to the two explosions in Riyadh on both the internal and external aspects. Most important amongst these is the awareness of the people to the significance of the American occupation of the country of the two sacred mosques, and that the original decrees of the regime are a reflection of the wishes of the American occupiers. So the people became aware that their main problems were caused by the American occupiers and their puppets in the Saudi regime, whether this was from the religious aspect or from other aspects in their everyday lives. The sympathies of the people with the working scholars who had been imprisoned also increased as has their understanding of their advises and guidance which led the people to support the general rectification movement which is led by the scholars and the callers to Islam. This movement - with the bounty of Allah - is increasing in power and in supporters day after day at the expense of the regime. The sympathy with these missions at the civil and military levels were great, as also the sympathies of the Muslim world with the struggle against the Americans.

As for the relationship between the regime and the American occupiers, these operations have embarrassed both sides and have led to the exchange of accusations between them. So we have the Americans stating that the causes of the explosions are the bad policies of the regime and the corruption of members of the ruling family, and the regime is accusing the Americans of exceeding their authority by taking advantage of the regime and forcing it to enter into military and civil contracts which are beyond its means, which led to great economic slide which has effected the people. In addition to this is the behaviour of the Americans with crudeness and

3

arrogance with the Saudi army and their general behaviour with citizens, and the privileges which the Americans enjoy in distinction from the Saudi forces.

These missions also paved the way for the raising of the voices of opposition against the American occupation from within the ruling family and the armed forces; in fact we can say that the remaining Gulf countries have been effected to the same degree, and that the voices of opposition to the American occupation have begun to be heard at the level of the ruling families and the governments of the Cooperative Council of Gulf countries. The differences in outlooks between the Americans and the Gulf states has appeared for the first time since the second Gulf war. This was during the conference of the ministers of external affairs of the countries of the cooperative council of Gulf states which was held in Riyadh to look into the American missile aggression against Iraq. These differences are nothing more than a sign of the strain which has eventuated in the relationship between America and the countries of the region in the footsteps of the Jihad missions against the Americans in Riyadh and as a result of the fear of these regimes that their own lands might witness similar Jihad missions.

Q: It was observed that the American and Saudi officials tried to link the latest operations to some foreign countries. What is behind these attempts?

A result of the increasing reaction of the people against the American occupation and the great sympathy with the Jihad missions against the Americans is the eagerness of the Americans and the Saudis to propagate false information to disperse these sympathies. This can be witnessed in their statements that some of the countries in the region were behind the Jihad missions inside the country of the two sacred mosques, however the people are aware that this is an internal Islamic movement against the American occupation which is revealing itself in the most clear picture after the killing of the four champions who performed the Riyadh operation, the ones concerning whom, we ask Allah to accept amongst the martyrs.

It has become routine policy for countries upon facing an internal calamity is to lay the responsibility on an external country. Before the puppetry of the Arabic countries to America became plainly obvious, the security sections never hesitated to accuse any rectifying Islamic movement to be a puppet to America and Israel.

Q: What are the regime's choices with regards to the Muslim uprising, and what are your expectations for the future?

There are several choices for the regime, one of these is reconciliation with all the different sections of the public, by releasing the scholars, and offering essential changes, the most important of these is to bring back Islamic law, and to practise real Shura (consultative government). The regime may resort to this choice after finding itself in the position of a morsel of food for the Americans to take, after the enmity has been stirred with their people. These people today feel that the Americans have exceeded their limits both politically and economically, the regime now knows that the public are aware that their sovereignty is shared. This was particularly evident in the recent period through the American press statements which give justification to the American occupation which only exists to rob the wealth of the people to the benefit of the Americans. This option is dependent on the agreement of the people who hold the solution and have the ability to effect change, at the forefront of these would be the honest scholars.

As for the other option, this is a very difficult and dangerous one for the regime, and this involves an escalation in the confrontation between the Muslim people and the American occupiers and to confront the economic hemorrhage. Its most important goal would be to change the current regime, with the permission of Allah.

Q: As a part of the furious international campaign against the Jihad movement, you were personally the target of a prejudiced attack, which accused you of financing terrorism and being part of an international terrorist organisation. What do you have to say about that?

After the end of the cold war, America escalated its campaign against the Muslim world in its entirety, aiming to get rid of Islam itself. Its main focus in this was to target the scholars and the reformers who were enlightening the people to the dangers of the Judeo - American alliance, and they also targeted the Mujahideen. We also have been hit with some of the traces of this campaign as we were accused of funding terrorism, and being members of an international terrorist organisation. Their aims in making these allegations were to place psychological pressure on the Mujahideen and their supporters so that they would forsake the obligation of Jihad and the resistance of oppression and American Israeli occupation of Islamic sacred lands. However, our gratitude to Allah, their campaign was not successful, as terrorising the American occupiers is a religious and logical obligation. We are grateful to Allah Most Exalted in that He has facilitated Jihad in His cause for us, against the Americo - Israeli attacks on the Islamic sanctities.

As for their accusations of terrorising the innocent, the children, and the women, these are in the category "accusing others with their own affliction in order to fool the masses". The evidence overwhelmingly shows America and Israel killing the weaker men, women, and children in the Muslim world and elsewhere. A few examples of this are seen in the recent Qana massacre in Lebanon, and the death of more than six hundred thousands (600,000) Iraqi children because of the shortage of food and medicine which resulted from the boycotts and sanctions against the Muslim Iraqi people, also their withholding of arms from the Muslims of Bosnian Hercegovina leaving them prey to the Christian Serbians who massacred and raped in a manner not seen in contemporary history. Not to forget the dropping of the H bombs on cities with their entire populations of children, elderly, and women, on purpose, and in a premeditated manner as was the case with Hiroshima and Nakazagki. Then, killing hundreds of thousands of children in Iraq, and whose numbers (of dead) continue to increase as a result of the sanctions. Despite the continuing American occupation of the country of the two sacred mosques, America continues to claim that it is upholding the banner of freedom and humanity, whilst these deeds which they did, you would find that the most ravenous of animals would not descend to.

As for what America accuses us of, of killing the innocent people, they have not been able to offer any evidence, despite the magnitude of their expenditure on their intelligence services. Despite what our history is witnessing in the Afghan phase of the Jihad. This was also unstained with any blood of innocent people, despite the inhuman Russian campaign against our women, our children, and our brothers in Afghanistan... Similar is our history with respect to our differences with the Saudi regime, all that has been proved is our joy at the killing of the American Soldiers in Riyadh and Khobar, and these are the sentiments of every Muslim. Our encouragement and call to Muslims to enter Jihad against the American and the Israeli occupiers are actions which we are engaging in as religious obligations. Allah Most High has commanded us in many verses of the Qur`an to fight in His path and to urge the believers to do so. Of these are His words: *"Fight in the path of Allah, you are not charged with the responsibility except for yourself, and urge the believers, lest Allah restrain the might of the rejectors, and Allah is stronger in might and stronger in inflicting punishment."* and His words: *"And what is it with you that you do not fight in the path of Allah, whilst the weak amongst the men, and the women, and the children who say: our Lord take us out of this town the people of which are oppressive, and make for us from You a protecting friend and make for us from You a succourer",* and His words: *"So if you meet those who reject, then strike the necks..."* We have given an oath to Allah to continue in the struggle as long as we have blood pumping in our veins or a seeing eye, and we beg of Allah to accept and to grant a good ending for us and for all the Muslims.

Q: Some media sources mentioned that the Afghan government demanded that you leave the country. How true is this?

The Afghan government has not asked us to leave the country... All gratitude to Allah, our relationship with our brother Mujahideen in Afghanistan is a deep and broad relationship where blood and sweat have mixed as have the links over long years of struggle against the Soviets, it is not a passing relationship, nor one based on personal interests.

They are committed to support the religion approved by Allah, and that country remains as the Muslims have known it, a strong fort for Islam, and its people are amongst the most protective of the religion approved by Allah, and the keenest to fulfil His laws and to establish an Islamic state.

That passing phase of infighting has saddened us as it has saddened all the Muslims, however, we wish to indicate that the picture of events as painted by the international press is grossly distorted, and that this infighting is much smaller and less fierce than what Muslims on the outside may imagine, and that most of the country is living a normal peaceful life; apart from some petty crimes here and there as some elements attempt to create corruption under cover of the disputes amongst some of the groups. We our hoping that Afghanistan would regain very soon - God willing - its Islamic position which would befit its history of Jihad.

Q: What is the responsibility of the Muslim populations towards the international campaign against Islam?

What bears no doubt in this fierce Judao - Christian campaign against the Muslim world, the likes of which has never been seen before, is that the Muslims must prepare all the possible might to repel the enemy on the military, economic, missionary, and all other areas. It is crucial for us to be patient and to cooperate in righteousness and piety and to raise awareness to the fact that the highest priority, after faith is to repel the incursive enemy which corrupts the religion and the world, and nothing deserves a higher priority after faith, as the scholars have declared, for this cause, it is crucial to overlook many of the issues of bickering in order to unite our ranks so that we can repel the greater Kufr.

All must move giving life to the words of the Most High: **"Indeed this, your community, is one community, and I am your Lord, so worship me"** and that they should not be like those whom Allah has described with His words: **"Indeed those who have divided their religion and became schisms, you are not of them in any way."** It is essential to volunteer and not to bicker, and the Muslim should not belittle righteousness in any way, the messenger (peace and blessings upon him) said: *"Whoever believes in Allah and the last day must speak good or not speak at all."* and they must heed the words of the messenger (peace and blessings upon him) when they move: *"Inform and do not repel, and make it easy and do not make it difficult."*.. And we ask Allah to give this community the guidance to exalt the people who obey Him and humiliate those who disobey Him, and to give us a rule where decency is commanded and evil is forbidden. O Allah bless Mohammad, Your servant and messenger, and his family, and companions, and give them peace... All gratitude to Allah the Lord of the worlds.

United States Indictments

MOHAMED RASHED DAOUD AL-'OWHALI

Et al.,

Indictment

INTRODUCTION

The Grand Jury charges:

COUNTS ONE THROUGH SIX:

CONSPIRACIES TO MURDER, BOMB AND MAIM

COUNT ONE:

CONSPIRACY TO KILL UNITED STATES NATIONALS

Overt Acts

12.   In furtherance of said conspiracy, and to effect the illegal objects thereof, the following overt acts, among others, were committed:

The Provision of Guesthouses and Training Camps

a.   At various times from at least as early as 1989, the defendant USAMA BIN LADEN, and others known and unknown, provided training camps and guesthouses in various areas, including Afghanistan, Pakistan, the Sudan, Somalia and Kenya for the use of al Qaeda and its affiliated groups.

The Recruitment of American Citizens

b.   At various times from at least as early as 1989, the defendant
USAMA BIN LADEN, and others known and unknown, made efforts to recruit United
States citizens, including the defendant WAHID EL HAGE, to help al Qaeda in order to
utilize the American citizens for travel throughout the Western world to deliver messages
and engage in financial transactions for the benefit of al Qaeda and its affiliated groups
and to help carry out operations;

Financial and Business Dealings

d.   …The defendants USAMA BIN LADEN and MAMDOUH
MAHMUD SALIM, and others…engaged in financial and business transactions on
behalf of al Qaeda including … purchasing land for training camps; purchasing
warehouses for storage of items, including explosives; purchasing communications and
electronics equipment; transferring funds between corporate accounts; and transporting
currency and weapons to members of al Qaeda and its associated terrorist organizations
in various countries throughout the world.

Establishment of Business in the Sudan

f.   Following al Qaeda's move to the Sudan, the defendant USAMA
BIN LADEN established a headquarters in the Riyadh section of Khartoum. USAMA
BIN LADEN also established a series of businesses in the Sudan…. These companies
were operated provide income to support al Qaeda and to provide cover for the
procurement of explosives, weapons and chemicals and for the travel of al Qaeda
operatives.

The Fatwahs Against American Troops in Saudi Arabia and Yemen

h.   …USAMA BIN LADEN … working together with members of
the fatwah committee of al Qaeda, disseminated fatwahs (rulings on Islamic law) to

members and associates of al Qaeda that the United States forces stationed on the Saudi Arabian peninsula, including both Saudi Arabia and Yemen, should be attacked;

The Fatwah Against American Troops in Somalia

m.   At various times from in or about 1992 until in or about 1993, the defendant USAMA BIN LADEN, working together with members of the fatwah committee of al Qaeda, disseminated fatwahs to other members and associates of al Qaeda that the United States forces stationed in the Horn of Africa, including Somalia, should be attacked.

n.   On various occasions in or about 1993, the defendant MAMDOUH MAHMUD SALIM lectured al Qaeda members that the United States forces do not belong in any Arab lands, and that the presence of the United Nations forces in Somalia was a reflection of the United States' plans to attack the Muslim world;

The Establishment of the Kenya Base of Operations

r.   In or about 1993, various members of al Qaeda, including the defendant KHALID AL FAWWAZ, began to establish businesses (including the business "Asma Limited,") and residences in Kenya, particularly in Nairobi;

The Attacks on the United States Forces in Somalia

w.   On October 3 and 4, 1993, in Mogadishu, Somalia, persons who had been trained by al Qaeda ... participated in an attack on United States military personnel serving in Somalia as part of Operation Restore Hope, which attack resulted in the killing of 18 United States Army personnel....

The Shipment of Weapons and explosives to Saudi Arabia

x.   On at least two occasions in the period from in or about 1992 until in or about 1995, members of al Qaeda transported weapons and explosives from Khartoum in the Sudan to the coastal city of Port Sudan for transshipment to the Saudi Arabian peninsula using vehicles associated with Usama Bin Laden's businesses;

The Fatwah Regarding Deaths of Nonbelievers

y.   On various occasions the defendant MAMDOUH MAHMUD SALIM advised other members of al Qaeda that it was Islamically proper to engage in violent actions against "infidels" (nonbelievers), even if others might be killed by such actions, because if the others were "innocent, they would go to paradise, and if they were not "innocent," they deserved to die;

The August 1996 Declaration of War

tt.   On or about July 31, 1996, the defendant KHALID AL FAWWAZ created, using a computer in his residence in London, England, a file entitled "the Message";

uu.   ..."Message from Usamah Bin-Muhammad Bin-Laden to His Muslim Brothers in the Whole World and Especially in the Arabian Peninsula: Declaration of Jihad Against the Americans Occupying the Land of the Two Holy Mosques; Expel the Heretics from the Arabian Peninsula" (hereafter the "Declaration of Jihad") was disseminated;

El Hage Lies to the Grand Jury in September 1997

vvv.   On or about September 24, 1997, in the Southern District of New York, the defendant WADIH EL HAGE made false statements concerning the nature of his contacts with al Qaeda and Egyptian Islamic Jihad to a federal Grand Jury conducting an investigation of al Qaeda;

The February 1998 Fatwah Against American Civilians

Al Zawahiri Appoints Deputies and Announces Draft Fatwah

ffff.   In February 1998, the defendants USAMA BIN LADEN and AYMAN AL ZAWAHIRI endorsed a fatwah under the banner of the "International Islamic Front for Jihad on the Jews and Crusaders." This fatwah, published in the publication Al-Quds al'Arabi on February 23, 1998, stated that Muslims should kill Americans — including civilians — anywhere they can be found;

iiii.   On or about May 7, 1998, the defendant MUHAMMAD ATEF, a/k/a "Abu Hafs," sent to the defendant KHALID AL FAWWAZ a letter discussing the endorsement by USAMA BIN LADEN of a fatwah issued by the "Ulema Union of Afghanistan" which termed the United States Army the "enemies of Islam" and declared a jihad against the United States and its followers, and defendant MUHAMMAD ATEF suggested how KHALID AL FAWWAZ should have the fatwah published;

Bin Laden Endorses the Nuclear Bomb of Islam

kkkk.   On or about May 29, 1998, the defendant USAMA BIN LADEN issued a statement entitled "The Nuclear Bomb of Islam," under the banner of the "International Islamic Front for Fighting Jews and Crusaders," in which he stated that "it is the duty of the Muslims to prepare as much force as possible to terrorize enemies of God";

The May 1998 Press Conference

qqqq.   In the days immediately following a May 1998 press interview, the defendant USAMA BIN LADEN held a press conference in Khost, Afghanistan, attended

also by the defendants KUHAMMAD ATEF and MOHAMED RADHED DAOUD AL-
'OWHALI, where USAMA BIN LADEN repeated his intention to kill Americans;

The Bombing in Nairobi

hhhhhh.   On August 7, 1998, beginning at approximately 9:30 a.m.
local time, the defendant FAZUL ABDULLAH MOHAMMED drove a pick-up truck
from the villa located at 43 New Runda Estates to the vicinity of the United States
Embassy in Nairobi, Kenya, while the defendant MOHAMED RASHED DAOUD AL-
'OWHALI rode in the Nairobi Bomb Truck driven by "Azzam" (a Saudi national)
containing a large bomb to the United States Embassy in Nairobi, Kenya. The defendant
MOHAMED RASHED DAOUD AL-'OWHALI possessed four stun-grenade type
devices, a 9 millimeter Beretta handgun, bullets, and keys to the padlocks on the Nairobi
Bomb Truck;

iiiiii.   On August 7, 1998, at approximately 10:30 a.m., the defendant
MOHAMED RASHED DAOUD AL-'OWHALI got out of the Nairobi Bomb Truck as it
approached the rear of the Embassy building and brandished a stun grenade before
throwing it in the direction of a security guard and then seeking to flee;

jjjjjj.   On August 7, 1998, at approximately 10:30 a.m., "Azzam" drove
the Nairobi Bomb Truck to the rear of the Embassy building and fired a handgun at the
windows of the embassy building;

kkkkkk.   On August 7, 1998, at approximately 10:30 a.m., "Azzam"
detonated the explosive device contained in the Nairobi Bomb Truck at a location near
the rear of the Embassy building, demolishing a multi-story secretarial college and
severely damaging the United State Embassy building and the Cooperative Bank
building, causing a total of more than 213 deaths, as well as injuries to more than 4,500
people, including citizens of Kenya and the United States;

llllll.   Following the August 7, 1998, bombing of the Embassy building in Nairobi, the defendant MOHAMED RASHED DAOUD AL-'OWHALI sought to secrete bullets and keys to the padlock on the Nairobi Bomb Truck in a hospital clinic in Nairobi;

The Dar es Salaam Bombing

mmmmmm.   On or about August 7, 1998, the defendant KHALFAN KHAMIS MOHAMED accompanied "Ahmed the German," an Egyptian national named as a co-conspirator but not as a defendant herein, in the Dar es Salaam Bomb Truck during a portion of the ride to the United States Embassy;

nnnnnn.   On August 7, 1998, at approximately 10:40 a.m., "Ahmed the German" detonated an explosive device contained, along with oxygen and acetylene tanks and truck batteries, in the Dar es Salaam Bomb Truck in the vicinity of the United States Embassy building located in Dar es Salaam, Tanzania, severely damaging the United States Embassy building and causing the deaths of at least 11 persons, including Tanzanian citizens, on the Embassy property, as well as injuries to at least 85 people;

oooooo.   On or about August 7 and August 8, 1998, the defendants ADEL ABDEL BARY and IBRAHIM EIDAROUS participated in the dissemination of claims of responsibility for the bombings of the American embassies in the name of "Islamic Army for the Liberation of the Holy Places" to media organizations in Paris, France; Doha, Qatar; and Dubai, United Arab Emirates;

El Hage Lies to the FBI in August 1998

yyyyyy.   On or about August 20, 1998, in Texas, the defendant WADIH EL HAGE made false statements concerning the nature of his contacts with al Qaeda to Special Agents of the FBI conducting a criminal investigation of al Qaeda, Egyptian Islamic Jihad, and the August 1998 bombings in Africa;

El Hage Lies to the Grand Jury in September 1998

        bbbbbbb.   On or about September 16, 1998, in the Southern District of New York, the defendant WADIH EL HAGE made false statements concerning the nature of his contacts with al Qaeda to a federal Grand Jury conducting an investigation of al Qaeda. Egyptian Islamic Jihad, and the August 1998 bombings in Africa;

Usama bin Laden Issues Further Threats in June 1999

        eeeeeeee.   In or about June 1999, in an interview with an Arabic-language television station, defendant USAMA BIN LADEN issued a further threat indicating that all American males should be killed.

COUNTS TWO HUNDRED EIGHTY-SEVEN THROUGH THREE HUNDRED EIGHT: PERJURY BEFORE FEDERAL GRAND JURIES AND FALSE STATEMENTS

Background

64. ...By September 1997, the Grand Jury investigation focused, in part, upon (i) the structure and operational status of al Qaeda in countries including the Sudan, Saudi Arabia, Egypt, Yemen, Somalia, Eritrea, Afghanistan, Pakistan, Bosnia, Croatia, Algeria, Tunisia, Lebanon, the Philippines, Tajikistan and Azerbaijan, and the Chechnya region of Russia and the Kashmiri region of India, as well as in Kenya and the United States;

65.   It was material to the Grand Jury sitting in the Southern District of New York to ascertain, among other things:

        (1) the tactical goals, and corresponding terrorism targets, of Usama Bin Laden and al Qaeda;

(2) the nature and timing of various statements, public and private, where Usama Bin Laden indicated that the United States was an enemy of al Qaeda and should be attacked;

(3) the identities, code names, aliases and whereabouts of any al Qaeda members and associates;

(4) the names of persons with whom the defendant WADIH EL HAGE associated while living in the Sudan and Kenya and while traveling in Pakistan and Afghanistan;

(5) the names of persons with whom the defendant WADIH EL HAGE associated while living in Tucson, Arizona, and Arlington, Texas, and during his visits to New York;

(6) the nature of the role, if any, played by the defendant WADIH EL HAGE in the murder of Rashad Khalifa in Tucson, Arizona, in 1990 and the identity of the person from New York who visited WADIH EL HAGE in Tucson prior to the murder;

(7) the nature of the relationship between the defendant WADIH EL HAGE and Mustafa Elnore, a/k/a "Mustafa Saif," named as a co-conspirator but not as a defendant herein;

(8) the nature and extent of the defendant WADIH EL HAGE's contacts with Usama bin Laden, Muhammad Atef, Khaled Al Fawwaz and Ali Mohamed as well as with "Abu Ubaidah al Banshiri," particularly in the period from 1993 through the fall of 1997;

(9) the role played by Usama Bin Laden and the members and associates of the al Qaeda organization, particularly to include the defendants WADIH EL HAGE, Muhammad Atef, as well as Ali Mohamed and "Abu Ubaidah al Banshiri," in the provision of logistical support and training....

68.　Following the appearance of the defendant WADIH EL HAGE before the Grand Jury in September 1997...the Grand Jury's investigation focused on... (i) the February 1998 fatwah signed by Usama Bin Laden, Ayman al Zawahiri and others under the banner of the "International Islamic Front for Jihad on the Jews and Crusaders," stating that Muslims should kill Americans — including civilians — anywhere in the world where they can be found; (ii) subsequent televised threats issued by Usama Bin Laden in May 1998 that his group did not distinguish between military and civilian personnel; (iii) the August 7, 1998, bombing of the United States Embassy in Nairobi, Kenya, which resulted in the deaths of at least 213 persons, including 12 Americans and the wounding of more than 4500 people; (iv) the nearly simultaneous August 7, 1998, bombing of the United States Embassy in Dar es Salaam, Tanzania, which resulted in the death of 11 persons and the wounding of more than 85 persons; (v) the meaning of certain documents recovered in searches conducted in Nairobi, Kenya, in August 1998, following the bombings, which bore the name and code name of WADIH EL HAGE, as well as code names for other al Qaeda members and associates; and (vi) the extent to which WADIH EL HAGE's international travels concerned efforts to procure chemical weapons and their components on behalf of Usama Bin Laden and Mamdouh Mahmud Salim.

New York Trial Testimony

UNITED STATES OF AMERICA V. USAMA BIN LADEN, et al.

United States District Court
Southern District of New York
February 14, 2001 (Day 3 of trial)
10:30 AM

Testimony of prosecution witness Jamal Ahmed Al-Fadl (a/k/a Confidential Source-1 [CS-1])

Questioner: Patrick Fitzgerald, Assistant United States Attorney

(Transcript of trial from http://www.cryptome.org. Edited by author for appendix.)

MR. FITZGERALD: During the time you were involved with al Qaida, did there come a time when you became involved in an attempt to purchase uranium?

MR. AL-FADL: Yes.

MR. FITZGERALD: Can you tell us when that was?

MR. AL-FADL: That's area of '94 or end of '93.

MR. FITZGERALD: Can you tell us how you came to be involved in the purchase of uranium?

MR. AL-FADL: I remember Abu Fadhl al Makkee, he call me and he told me we hear somebody in Khartoum, he got uranium, and we need you to go and study that, is that true or not.

MR. FITZGERALD: The person who told you was Abu Fadhl al Makkee?

MR. AL-FADL: Yes.
...
MR. FITZGERALD: What happened when you went to that street in Khartoum?

MR. AL-FADL: ..., he told me, are you serious? You want uranium? I tell him yes. I know people, they very serious, and they want to buy it. And he told me did the money ready, and I say what they need. They need the information about uranium, they want to know which quality, which the country make it, and after that we going to talk with you about the price. He say I going to give you this information in a paper, and we need $1,500,000, and everything go well we need it outside. We need the money outside of Sudan.

MR. FITZGERALD: And the price was how much?

1

MR. AL-FADL: He say he need $1,500,000. And he say this is for the uranium. But he need commission for himself, and he need commission for Salah Abdel al Mobruk.

MR. FITZGERALD: What happened then?

MR. AL-FADL: After that he tell me how you going to check it? I tell him I don't know, I have to go to those people and I tell them what you tell me and I give you answer for that.

MR. FITZGERALD: What happened that?

MR. AL-FADL: After that I went to Abdallah al Yemeni and I told him what I got. He told me go to Abu Fadhl al Makkee and told him about what you got, what you have information, and I went to Abu Fadhl al Makkee and I told him, and he say you have to go to Abu Rida al Suri and sit down with him and told him, and he going to go with you after that.
    I went to ... Khartoum City, and I told him about the whole information, and he say tell him we have our machine, electric machine, we going to check the uranium but first we want to see and we want information. We want to see the cylinder and we want to need information about the quality and which country it make. And he tell me, he give me a little paper and he tell me give him this paper and this information we need...

MR. FITZGERALD: ... When you took the information you went back to Fadhl Shaheedin, and what did you do then?

MR. AL-FADL: Fadhl told me give me few days ...After that, I remember Fadhl, he call me and he tell me -- he give me a date. He tell me in that day, 10:00 in the morning, I need you near Khartoum Bank in Jambourah Street. He told me if you Abu Rida al Suri with you, that's good. I told him we don't have to bring Abu Rida, we just want ... information. He told me no, maybe you go to see the cylinder but we don't know. I went back to Abu Rida and I told him that. He say I don't mind, yeah, I going to come in that time.

MR. FITZGERALD: Did you go to the meeting?...You went with Fadl al Shaheedin and Abu Rida al Suri in a jeep to Khartoum north to a town called Bait al Mal...?

MR. AL-FADL: And we went over there and we, they took us inside house in Bait al Mal, and after few minutes they bring a big bag and they open it, and it cylinder, like this tall.

MR. FITZGERALD: For the record, the witness is indicating approximately two to three feet.

MR. AL-FADL: It's like this tall, I believe. And they give us a paper before that, and Abu Rida al Suri, I remember he took the paper and it's a lot written in the cylinder. It's like --

MR. FITZGERALD: Tell the word that you are saying to the interpreter.

2

MR. AL-FADL: (Through the interpreter) The information was like engraved. (Continuing in English) Abu Rida al Suri looked to his paper and he looked to the cylinder, and after that he say OK, that is good... And we left the house, and few days later he told me --

THE COURT: Who told you?

MR. AL-FADL: Abu Rida al Suri, he told me go to Fadl al Shaheedin and tell him we want to see Basheer again.

MR. FITZGERALD: So Abu Rida al Suri told you to go to Fadl al Shaheedin and tell him that who wanted to meet?

MR. AL-FADL: He told me go to Basheer and tell him we need another meeting, and in the same time he give me the paper we got from Dashoor about the information, and he told me I needed to take this paper to Abu Hajer and give him this paper, and whatever he tell you, or if he don't say anything, that's fine.

MR. FITZGERALD: So he told you to take the paper to Abu Hajer. What did you do?

MR. AL-FADL: I went to Abu Hajer in his house and I give him the paper and he need it and he say OK.

MR. FITZGERALD: What was on the paper?

MR. AL-FADL: It's information, I remember it say South Africa and serial number and quality something. It's all in English. So I don't remember all the what in the paper.

MR. FITZGERALD: What happened when you gave this paper to Abu Hajer?

MR. AL-FADL: He read it and he say OK, he say go back to Abu Rida al-Suri

MR. FITZGERALD: What happened then?

MR. AL-FADL: After that, I followed, he make a meeting with me and Basheer, and we told Basheer, the people they like to buy the cylinder. And he told me how you going to check it, and I told him what Abu Rida al Suri tell me, they wait for machine come from outside to check it.

MR. FITZGERALD: Did Abu Rida al Suri tell you where the machine to test the uranium was coming from?

MR. AL-FADL: He told me going to come from Kenya.

MR. FITZGERALD: Did you tell that to Basheer?

MR. AL-FADL: Yes, and he ask me how long is going to take. I tell him I don't know.

MR. FITZGERALD: What happened that?

MR. AL-FADL: After that, after few days Abu Fadl al Shahideen, he told me he make meeting between Abu Rida al Suri and Salah Abdel al-Mobruk.

MR. FITZGERALD: So the meeting was between Abu Rida al Suri and Salah Abdel al Mobruk.

MR. AL-FADL: And I tell him I don't know that, and he say you have to talk with Abu Rida al Suri. And I told him you don't want me no more go for this, and he say yes, everything fine, you did great job, and he give me $10,000.

MR. FITZGERALD: Did he tell you what the $10,000 he gave you was for?

MR. AL-FADL: He says this is for what you did, and he told me don't... tell anybody, you did great job, we going to check it and everything be fine...

MR. FITZGERALD: After that, did you take any more role in this attempt to buy uranium? Did you do anything else?

MR. AL-FADL: No.

MR. FITZGERALD: Did they ever tell you whether in fact they bought that uranium?

MR. AL-FADL: No, but I hear they check it in Hilat Koko.

MR. BAUGH (David P. Baugh, Attorney for defendant Mohamed Rashed Daoud Al-'Owhali): Objection, your Honor, to what he heard.

MR. FITZGERALD: We consent to that.

MR. FITZGERALD: ... After that, did you hear anything more about what happened to the uranium? Yes or no.

MR. AL-FADL: Yes.

MR. FITZGERALD: Where did you have a conversation with ... who told you what happened to the uranium?...What were the circumstances under which this person ...told you about what happened to the uranium?

MR. AL-FADL: ...we talk about the south Sudan and the army, they lose a lot of fighting because of the rain and the people in south Sudan do better in the rain against the government, and we talk about the chemical weapons, they try to build it to win the war in south Sudan. After that, he say you did great job about the uranium and they going to check it in Hilat Koko.

MR. FITZGERALD: Did you ever hear whether or not in fact they checked the uranium in Hilat Koko?

MR. AL-FADL: No...

UNITED STATES OF AMERICA V. USAMA BIN LADEN, et al.
United States District Court
Southern District of New York
February 14,2001 (Day 5 of trial)
10:30 AM

Testimony of prosecution witness Mr. Essam al-Ridi

Questioner: Patrick Fitzgerald, Assistant United States Attorney for the Southern District of New York

(Transcript of trial from http://www.cryptome.org. Edited by author for appendix.)

MR. FITZGERALD: ...Can you tell us what Wadih El Hage told you when he first contacted you?

MR. AL-RIDI: The interests of Usama Bin Laden in acquiring an airplane for Khartoum.

MR. FITZGERALD: And did you, did he tell you where Usama Bin Laden was living at the time?

MR. AL-RIDI. Yes.

MR. FITZGERALD: Where was he living?

MR. AL-RIDI: In Khartoum, Sudan.

MR. FITZGERALD: And what did he tell you about the airplane that he wished you to purchase for Usama Bin Laden?

MR. AL-RIDI: The price range within 350,000 US, and that is a range of about a little bit over two thousand miles.

MR. FITZGERALD: And did you have any further discussions with him about the financial arrangements for purchasing this airplane?

MR. AL-RIDI: Yes.

MR. FITZGERALD: What was that discussion?

MR. AL-RIDI: Once I located an airplane with that price and that range, I've called Wadih and specifically told him, it's 350,000 and I'll be offered 9 percent from the dealer, the owner of the

1

airplane… (El-Hage and Bin Laden) came later with a different price. Instead of 350, anything less than 250.

MR. FITZGERALD: And what did he tell you about the changed price?

MR. AL-RIDI: They wanted something within the 250,000 or less, and my response was, you'll never get a used jet aircraft for that price that will do the range that you want.

MR. FITZGERALD: And what happened then?

MR. AL-RIDI: Actually, they came with that final decision, it doesn't matter. This is the budget and let's try to work with that budget.

MR. FITZGERALD: Was there any discussion of the reason why the range for the plane had to be two thousand miles?

MR. AL-RIDI: Yes.

MR. FITZGERALD: Can you tell us what was said?

MR. AL-RIDI: They have some goods of their own they want to ship from Peshawar to Khartoum.

MR. FITZGERALD: And first of all, who is "they"?

MR. AL-RIDI: Again, I'm referring to Wadih and Usama.

MR. FITZGERALD: And did he tell you what the goods were that he wanted to ship from Peshawar to Khartoum?

MR. AL-RIDI: Yes.

MR. FITZGERALD: What were they?

MR. AL-RIDI: Stinger missiles.

MR. FITZGERALD: And when he told you they wanted to ship Stinger missiles from Peshawar to Khartoum, what did you say?

MR. AL-RIDI: I said it's possible as long as we have arrangements from the departing country to the arriving country.

MR. FITZGERALD: And what do you mean by that?

MR. AL-RIDI: I meant the legality, because it's clearly air policy.

MR. FITZGERALD: Did you discuss this with Wadih?

MR. AL-RIDI: Yes.

MR. FITZGERALD: Tell us what you told him about the legality of shipping the Stingers from Peshawar to Khartoum?

MR. AL-RIDI: That we have to have a legal permit to depart Peshawar with that equipment on board, and the legal permit to land in Khartoum, which is not a problem because they could ally people in Peshawar and also in Khartoum. However, the problem with allies, once we have to divert or land for any fuel or any emergency in the countries in between, then it will be definitely exposed and then it will be absolutely a chaos.

MR. FITZGERALD: And what, if anything, did he say in response?

MR. AL-RIDI: Nothing in particular. I was just explaining to them technicalities.

MR. FITZGERALD: And did you have a further discussion after that conversation about shipping stinger missiles?

MR. AL-RIDI: I don't think so, no.

MR. FITZGERALD: Did you ever actually transport yourself stinger missiles from Peshawar to Khartoum?

MR. AL-RIDI: No.

MR. FITZGERALD: Did you find a plane for the price of less than $250,000?

MR. AL-RIDI: Yes.

MR. FITZGERALD: …And what was the price?

MR. AL-RIDI: 210,000…

MR. FITZGERALD: And where did the money come from to acquire the plane?

MR. AL-RIDI: From Khartoum.

MR. FITZGERALD: And approximately how much money came from Khartoum if you recall?

MR. AL-RIDI: About a total of 230, 230, around that figure.

MR. FITZGERALD: 230 dollars or 230,000 dollars?

MR. AL-RIDI: Thousand dollars...

...

MR. FITZGERALD: Did you actually fly the plane yourself from the United States to Khartoum?

MR. AL-RIDI: Yes, I did.

MR. FITZGERALD: How long did it actually take you to get there?

MR. AL-RIDI: About a week.

MR. FITZGERALD: Do you recall approximately when was that you flew the plane from the United States to Sudan?

MR. AL-RIDI: The early part of 1993.

MR. FITZGERALD: And what happened when you arrived in Khartoum with the plane?

MR. AL-RIDI: Nothing. I just parked the airplane, took permission in the civil aviation authorities there and I was met with Wadih and I'm not sure maybe another driver or so.

MR. FITZGERALD: And where did you go with Wadih and the driver?

MR. AL-RIDI: We went to Wadih's house.

MR. FITZGERALD: And what did you do there?

MR. AL-RIDI: Had lunch with him.

MR. FITZGERALD: Did there come a time when you met Usama Bin Laden on that trip?

MR. AL-RIDI: Yes.

MR. FITZGERALD: When was that?

MR. AL-RIDI: It must have been the same day, at night, we were offered dinners on his behalf.

MR. FITZGERALD: And where was the dinner held?

MR. AL-RIDI: At his guest house.

...

MR. FITZGERALD: Approximately how long had you stayed there?

MR. AL-RIDI: It must have been maybe three or four days. I'm not really sure.

MR. FITZGERALD: How did you get back to America once you left the plane there?

MR. AL-RIDI: I used KLM as my company...

MR. FITZGERALD: ...Did there come a time when you saw the airplane again?

MR. AL-RIDI: Yes...

MR. FITZGERALD: ...Can you tell us when that happened and how?

MR. AL-RIDI: I was asked later to come and do a trip to them from Khartoum to Nairobi.

MR. FITZGERALD: Who asked you to do that?

MR. AL-RIDI: Wadia.

MR. FITZGERALD: When he asked you to do it, where were you and where was he?

MR. AL-RIDI: I was in the U.S. and he was in Khartoum.

MR. FITZGERALD: And how long after you returned from delivering the airplane was it before you received this call from Wadia asking you to come back?

MR. AL-RIDI: It must have been few months because the aircraft was still in good condition.

MR. FITZGERALD: Was still in what kind of condition?

MR. AL-RIDI: Good condition, good flying condition.

MR. FITZGERALD: Did you go back?

MR. AL-RIDI: Yes, I did.

MR. FITZGERALD: What happened when you got back to Khartoum?

MR. AL-RIDI: Nothing. I just prepared the aircraft and flew between Khartoum and Nairobi...

MR. FITZGERALD: Who or what did you fly from Khartoum to Nairobi?

MR. AL-RIDI: I flew five gentlemens.

MR. FITZGERALD: Do you know the names of the people you flew?

MR. AL-RIDI: No.

MR. FITZGERALD: Can you describe what they look like?

MR. AL-RIDI: They're all Arabs, dressed differently.

MR. FITZGERALD: Could you describe their dress?

MR. AL-RIDI: Yes. A few were dressed in the Saudi outfit, some are dressed in Western and dressed in Yemeni outfit.

MR. FITZGERALD: And what happened when you flew these five people down to Nairobi?

MR. AL-RIDI: Nothing. Actually, we landed, they were escorted inside the terminal. Me and my first officer stayed at the tarmac for about maybe an hour and 15, an hour and a half to secure the aircraft and to have the Customs check the aircraft.

MR. FITZGERALD: How long did you stay in Nairobi?

MR. AL-RIDI: About maybe two nights.

MR. FITZGERALD: Where did you go then?

MR. AL-RIDI: We went back to Khartoum.

MR. FITZGERALD: When you went back, did you take the same five people back to Khartoum?

MR. AL-RIDI: No.

MR. FITZGERALD: Did anyone tell you where they went?

MR. AL-RIDI: No.

MR. FITZGERALD: Do you know what they were doing after they got off the airplane?

MR. AL-RIDI: No...

MR. FITZGERALD:... After you took this jet from Khartoum to Nairobi and Nairobi back to Khartoum, what did you do once you arrived back in Khartoum?

MR. AL-RIDI: I flew back to the U.S....

UNITED STATES OF AMERICA V. USAMA BIN LADEN, et al.
United States District Court
Southern District of New York
February 28, 2001 (Day 12 of trial)
9:50 AM

Testimony of prosecution witness FBI Special Agent John Michael Anticev

Questioner: Patrick Fitzgerald, Assistant United States Attorney

(Transcript of trial from http://www.cryptome.org. Edited by author for appendix.)

(Names in Italics are replacements of aliases of defendants used in testimony.)

MR. FITZGERALD: ...Let me make that two questions. Did he (Odeh) indicate during the course of the interview who he thought had bombed the American Embassy?

AGENT ANTICEV: That his cell, *Abdullah Ahmed Abdullah* and company.

MR. FITZGERALD: Did he indicate who he thought had built the bomb and where?

AGENT ANTICEV: He thought that it was *Fazul Abdullah Mohammed* and *Musin Musa Matwalli Atwah* building the bomb at *Fazul Abdullah Mohammed*'s house.

MR. FITZGERALD: That would be the bomb of the American Embassy in Nairobi?

AGENT ANTICEV: Yes.

MR. FITZGERALD: Did he indicate who he thought built the bomb for the embassy in Tanzania?

AGENT ANTICEV: He made a statement that he believed that *Musin Musa Matwalli Atwah* could have built that one, too.

MR. FITZGERALD: During the course of the interview, did Odeh indicate to you how he thought one could get explosives into Nairobi?

AGENT ANTICEV: Yes. He gave us a situation where explosives could be smuggled into Nairobi in boxes of lobsters.

MR. FITZGERALD: Did he indicate that in fact it was smuggled that way, or is that his indication of how they could have been smuggled?

AGENT ANTICEV: Could have been smuggled.

MR. FITZGERALD: Did Odeh during the interviews make comments to you what he thought of the actual bombing and how it was carried out?

AGENT ANTICEV: He thought it was a blunder. He blamed *Abdullah Ahmed Abdullah* for making a big mistake. He didn't like the fact that so many civilians and Kenyans were killed. He said that the bombing of Khobar Towers was a hundred times better and that the individuals who had the, who drove the truck with the explosives should have got it into the building or died trying.

MR. FITZGERALD: Before we continue, I think you were going to give an instruction.

THE COURT: With respect to the Khobar matter, the parties have stipulated that no defendants are charged with participating in the Khobar bombing or in conspiring with respect thereto.
That's a stipulation.

MR. FITZGERALD: Thank you, Judge.
Did Odeh tell you what he thought, how he thought the mistake had been made with regard to the bombing that caused so many civilians to be killed?

AGENT ANTICEV: Well, one, they couldn't get it into the building and, two, the bomb was in the back of a pickup truck. So, you imagine how a pickup truck is. The bomb is in the back. He said that the truck should have been backed into the target closely, okay, because the cab in front would act as a diversion for the explosion.
So what actually happened is the truck came in nose first and when the bomb went off, he said that the force of the explosion actually ricocheted for a second off the cab, which diverted the explosion and caused so much more damage in the area.

MR. FITZGERALD: So we're clear, what he's telling is you what he thinks the mistakes were that were made that would have caused the buildings nearby to be hit by the bomb explosion?

AGENT ANTICEV: Yes.

MR. FITZGERALD: During the time that you interviewed Mr. Odeh, did he indicate to you why it was that he was talking to you?

AGENT ANTICEV: Yes. He stated that the reason he was talking to us now was because the people that he was with were pushing him and pushing him and pushing him and they're all gone and he's left here facing big problems...

2

UNITED STATES OF AMERICA V. USAMA BIN LADEN, et al.

United States District Court
Southern District of New York
March 1, 2001 (Day 13 of trial)
9:50 AM

Testimony of prosecution witness The Honorable Prudence Bushnell, the former Ambassador of the United States of America to the Republic of Kenya

Questioner: Paul Butler, Assistant United States Attorney for the Southern District of New York

(Transcript of trial from http://www.cryptome.org. Edited by author for appendix.)

MR. BUTLER: ... Ambassador Bushnell, do you recall the morning of August 7, 1998?

AMBASSADOR BUSHNELL: Yes, I do.

MR. BUTLER: Did you go to the embassy that morning?

AMBASSADOR BUSHNELL: Yes. It was an ordinary Friday. I went to the embassy, about 8:00 arrived there.

MR. BUTLER: Do you recall where you were later on that morning?

AMBASSADOR BUSHNELL: I had a meeting in the Cooperative Bank Building with the Minister of Commerce... I was in the Cooperative Bank Building behind the embassy building.

MR. BUTLER: Do you recall approximately what time that meeting began?

AMBASSADOR BUSHNELL: That meeting began at 10:00 in the morning.

MR. BUTLER: Do you recall generally what floor you were on in the Cooperative Bank House?

AMBASSADOR BUSHNELL: It was on the top floor of the Cooperative Bank Building.

MR. BUTLER: Do you recall what happened after this meeting began, Ambassador Bushnell?

AMBASSADOR BUSHNELL: After about 15 or 20 minutes with the press, the minister dismissed the press... We had only -- we were maybe two or three, four minutes into the conversation when we all heard a very loud explosion. I turned to the minister and asked if there was construction going on in the area, because to me it sounded like the kind of explosion you would hear associated with construction. He said no.... And it was at that point that an enormous

1

explosion came. I was the last person out of my seat and had just taken a few steps before this huge explosion happened. I was thrown back, and although I didn't think at the time I was unconscious, I must have been because when I brought myself back to reality, I was sitting down with my hands over my head because the ceiling was falling down. I will never forget the rattling of a teacup, just kept rattling. I thought to myself that the building was going to collapse, that I was going to tumble down all those stories, and that I was going to die, and every cell in my body was just steeled toward waiting for the fall... I was alone in the room. The only other person present was a man who was prone, face down on the floor. I thought he was dead.

Almost simultaneously, one of my Department of Commerce colleagues came rushing into the room and the man who was prone on the floor raised his head. My colleague said Ambassador, we've got to get out of here...we climbed over the door into the stairwell, which had been blown into the stairwell.

MR. BUTLER: What did the top floor look like after you gained consciousness? What did you see around you?

AMBASSADOR BUSHNELL: The office was a mess because the ceiling had, part of the ceiling had fallen in, and the furniture was overturned and papers were scattered all over the place... But as we climbed over the door I saw someone's shoe and a great deal of blood. And then the reality of, the enormity of the blast began to hit.

MR. BUTLER: You said you made your way to the doorway. What happened after you made your way to the doorway?

AMBASSADOR BUSHNELL: We began to climb down the stairs very slowly, and at the upper floors there were not very many people, but as we got down, the further down we got the more and more people we found in the stairway, until we were a procession of human beings who were smashed together, going down those endless stairs.

There was no panic, which was amazing, and also something that probably saved a lot of lives.

I was also struck of the almost eerie silence. It was a very hushed procession. As people joined us from different floors, sometimes you would hear somebody yell out welcome. You could also hear some people who were praying. Some other people were singing hymns. Down we went. As we got to the lower floors, this huge procession of people, who were bleeding all over one another -- there was blood everywhere, on the banister, I could feel the person behind me bleeding on my hair and down my back. As we got to the lower floors the procession stopped, and somebody yelled out, there's a fire, hurry. We had stopped in the middle of smoke. That was the second time that day that I was fairly confident that I was going to die, and all I could think of was well, at least I'm not going to be burned alive, at least I will die from asphyxiation...

MR. BUTLER: ... So after you hit the point where the smoke was coming in, what happened after that?

AMBASSADOR BUSHNELL: Eventually we started walking down again very slowly. I will say that in this procession down, at one point a woman collapsed. I am not sure if she died or, I have no idea what happened to her, but she was passed down over my head and passed down. Now and again I would see the body of somebody and the body would be picked up and taken down.

Eventually we came towards the bottom. I had no idea that this was an explosion directed at anything but the bank building. My reality was simply inside that building. I kept thinking, all I have to do is get out of here and go back to my embassy, into the medical unit, because we had a medical unit, and somebody will take care of me.

My colleague and I came out of the front of the Cooperative Bank Building, and I saw what seemed like thousands of people across the street looking on. At that point my colleague said put your face down, the press is here, and literally pushed my face down. So the first thing I saw was what was on the street. A lot of glass, lot of glass, twisted pieces of charred metal. So I was stepping over an enormous amount of debris. As we came out and we came by our parking lot, what was our parking lot, I looked up and saw burning vehicles. I saw the charred remains of what was once a human being. I saw the back of the building completely ripped off and utter destruction, and I knew that no one was going to take care of me.

We came along the side of the building and were spotted by our security people, who started yelling get her out of here, get her out of here. I think there was a great deal of concern, as there often is, that there might be another attack. They didn't want the US ambassador, having found her alive they didn't want anything to happen. So I was literally pulled around the front of the building where we found a vehicle. I was pushed into the vehicle with my two colleagues. We had by that time found the second man from the Department of Commerce, both of whom were bleeding profusely. And I asked the driver to take me to a hotel rather than a hotel, because I very much needed to get to work, and I was afraid if we went to a hospital it would just take too long waiting in the emergency room.

MR. BUTLER: I would like to publish now Government's Exhibit 804A...Ambassador Bushnell, could you tell us what is depicted in Government's Exhibit 804A.

AMBASSADOR BUSHNELL: That is very likely -- that photograph was very likely taken after the bombing, because you can see the huge amount of smoke coming.

MR. BUTLER: Is this similar to the scene that you encountered once you got out of the Cooperative Bank House?

AMBASSADOR BUSHNELL: I was on the ground obviously, but yes, this was -- it was this kind of scene from a war...

MR. BUTLER: ... Why don't we go to Government's Exhibit 806F, which has been received in evidence.

Is this a photograph of you after the bombing, Ambassador Bushnell?

AMBASSADOR BUSHNELL: Yes. That was taken a day or so after the bombing. I had a number of bandages on my hands, again because I had my hand over my head. The debris came and hit hand and arms. I have absolutely no idea how I cut my lip, but there you are. I had stitches in my lip…

MR. BUTLER: …Did you go back to the embassy in the days following the bombing, Ambassador Bushnell?

AMBASSADOR BUSHNELL: The first time I went back to the embassy was the next day…the first time I was back in the building was Saturday morning.

MR. BUTLER: Did you pay several visits to the area of the embassy in the days and weeks following that?

AMBASSADOR BUSHNELL: For the subsequent months I was in the building very often.

MR. BUTLER: I would like to show you a series of photographs… What is depicted in Government's Exhibit A, Ambassador Bushnell?

AMBASSADOR BUSHNELL: That is an aerial view. You can see the Cooperative Bank Building, the tall building. You can see the embassy. What you will not see is the Ufundi House. Do you see the rubble in the corner between -- if you look at the embassy and you look to the left of the embassy, you can see some white rubble. That was once a seven-story building…

MR. BUTLER: …What is depicted in 805B, Ambassador?

AMBASSADOR BUSHNELL: Again, it's a shot down to the embassy building. If you will notice, virtually every window in the Cooperative Bank Building has been blown out. The embassy building itself looks pretty good from the outside. In fact, it was utter devastation on the inside and in the back… May I just say that the embassy had been built in the seventies to withstand an earthquake, which was why the outer walls managed to stay pretty much put.

MR. BUTLER: Looking at 805C, this again is a photograph of the embassy after the bombing, in the area?

AMBASSADOR BUSHNELL: That is correct. Again, what you are looking at, if you take as reference point the Cooperative Bank Building, you will see in the back face of the Cooperative Building the embassy, and again I will just point out that in the corner to the right of the embassy where you see the white rubble is what was once an office building filled with people…

MR. BUTLER: …You mentioned that there was damage to the interior of the embassy. Were you inside the embassy after the bombing?

AMBASSADOR BUSHNELL: As I said, the first time I went inside the embassy was the Saturday morning after the bombing.

MR. BUTLER: Did you take tours of some of the damage on the inside of the embassy?

AMBASSADOR BUSHNELL: I went throughout the embassy...

MR. BUTLER: ... Is this a picture of the interior of the embassy after the bombing?

AMBASSADOR BUSHNELL: That's correct. That is one of the hallways, I believe...

MR. BUTLER: ...Is that another photo of the interior of the embassy after the bombing?

AMBASSADOR BUSHNELL: That is correct. That is the inside of what used to be an office.

MR. BUTLER: And 809H.

AMBASSADOR BUSHNELL: Another office. Used to be...

MR. BUTLER: ...Do you recognize this as another photo of the interior of the embassy, Ambassador?

AMBASSADOR BUSHNELL: That's correct. Once again, that's an office in which people worked...

MR. BUTLER: ...Is this another photo of the interior of the embassy after the bombing?

AMBASSADOR BUSHNELL: Yes, it is, including a file cabinet with one of the drawers thrown open.

MR. BUTLER: If you look in the photo through the opening in the middle of the photo, do you see a building in the background? Do you recognize what that is?

AMBASSADOR BUSHNELL: That is the Cooperative Bank Building, so what you are seeing is a photo that is taken from inside the embassy out the back...

MR. BUTLER: ...Why don't we skip ahead to 809Y. Do you recognize this as another depiction of the interior of the embassy after the bombing?

AMBASSADOR BUSHNELL: That is correct, and you can see the blue sky between what was once a wall.

MR. BUTLER: Let's go to 809AZ. Again, do you recognize this as a photo of the damage to the interior of the embassy?

AMBASSADOR BUSHNELL: That is correct, and once again, the photo is taken from inside the building. You are looking at Ufundi House and what was once a wall, no longer there, caved in...

MR. BUTLER: ...Again, is there another photo of damage to the interior of the embassy?

AMBASSADOR BUSHNELL: That is correct. This is another office.

MR. BUTLER: No further questions, your Honor.

United States Perspectives: Selected Documents

ADDRESS BY PRESDIENT CLINTON
ON MILITARY ACTIONS AGAINST TERRORIST
SITES IN AFGHANISTAN AND SUDAN
ON AUGUST 20, 1998

August 20, 1998

Good afternoon. Today I ordered our Armed Forces to strike at terrorist-related facilities in Afghanistan and Sudan because of the imminent threat they presented to our national security.

I want to speak with you about the objective of this action and why it was necessary. Our target was terror. Our mission was clear, to strike at the network of radical groups affiliated with and funded by Usama bin Ladin, perhaps the preeminent organizer and financer of international terrorism in the world today.

The groups associated with him come from diverse places but share a hatred for democracy, a fanatical glorification of violence, and a horrible distortion of their religion to justify the murder of innocents. They have made the United-States their adversary precisely because of what we stand for and what we stand against.

A few months ago, and again this week, bin ladin publicly vowed to wage a terrorist war against America, saying, and I quote, " We do not differentiate between those dressed in military uniforms and civilians. They're all targets."

Their mission is murder and their history is bloody. In recent years, they killed American, Belgian, and Pakistani peacekeepers in Somalia. They plotted to assassinate the President of Egypt and the Pope. They planned to bomb six United States 747's over the Pacific. They bombed the Egyptian Embassy in Pakistan. They gunned down German tourists in Egypt.

The most recent terrorist events are fresh in our memory. Two weeks ago, 12 Americans and nearly Kenyans and Tanzanians lost their lives, and another 5000 were wounded, when our embassies in Nairobi and Dar es Salaam were bombed. There is convincing information from our intelligence community that the bin-Ladin terrorist network was responsible for these bombings. Based on this information, we have high confidence that the bombings were planned, financed, and carried out by the organization bin Ladin leads.

America has battled terrorism for many years. Where possible, we've used law enforcement and diplomatic tools to wage the fight. The long arm of American law has reached out around the world and brought trial those guilty of attacks in New York and Virginia and in the Pacific. We have quietly disrupted terrorist groups and foiled their plots. We have isolated countries that practice terrorism. We've worked to build an international coalition against terror.

But there have been and will be times when law enforcement and diplomatic tools are simply not enough, when our very national security is challenged, and when we must take extraordinary steps to protect the safety of our citizens. With compelling evidence that the bin Ladin network of terrorist groups was planning to mount further attacks against American and other freedom-loving people, I decided America must act.

And so this morning, based on the unanimous recommendation of my national security team, I ordered our Armed Forces to take action to counter an immediate threat from the bin Ladin network. Earlier today, the United States carried out simultaneous strikes against terrorist facilities and infrastructure in Afghanistan. Our forces targeted one of the most active terrorist bases in the world. It contained key elements of the bin Ladin network's infrastructure and has served as a training camp for literally thousands of terrorist leaders was to take place there today, thus underscoring the urgency of our actions.

Our forces also attacked a factory in Sudan associated with the bin Ladin network. The factory was involved in the production of materials for chemical weapons.

The United States does not take this action lightly. Afghanistan and Sudan have been warned for years to stop harboring and supporting these terrorist groups. But countries that persistently host terrorists have no right to be safe havens.

Let me express my gratitude to our intelligence and law enforcement agencies for their hard, good work. And let me express my pride in our Armed Forces who carried out this mission while making every possible effort to minimize the loss of innocent life.

I want you to understand, I want the world to understand that our actions today were not aimed against Islam, the faith of hundreds of millions of good, peace-loving people all around the world, including the United States. No religion condones the murder of innocent men, women, and children. But our actions were aimed at fanatics and killers who wrap murder in the cloak of righteousness and in so doing profane the great religion in whose name they claim to act.

My fellow Americans, our battle against terrorism did not begin with the bombing of our Embassies in Africa, nor will it end with today's strike. It will require strength, courage, and endurance. We will not yield to this threat. We will meet it, no matter how long it may take. This will be long, ongoing struggle between freedom and fanaticism, between the rule of law and terrorism. We must be prepared to do all that we can for as long as we must.

America is and will remain a target of terrorists precisely because we are leaders, because we act to advance peace, democracy, and basic human values, because we're the most open society on Earth, and because, as we have shown yet again, we take an uncompromising stand against terrorism.

But of this I am also sure: The risks from inaction, to America and the World, would be
far greater then action, for that would embolden our enemies, leaving their ability and
their willingness to strike us intact. In this case, we knew before our attack that these
groups already had planned further actions against us and others.

I want to reiterate: The United States wants peace, not conflict. We want to lift lives
around the world, not take them. We have worked for peace in Bosnia, in Northern
Ireland, In Haiti, in the Middle East and elsewhere. But in this day, no champion for
peace can succeed without a determination to fight terrorism. Let our actions today send
this message loud and clear: There is no expendable American targets; threw will be no
sanctuary for terrorists; we will defend our people, our interests, and our values; we will
help people of all faiths, in all parts of the world, who want to live free of fear and
violence. We will persist, and we will prevail.

Thank you. And may God bless our country.

February 4, 1999

Statement for the Record of
Louis J. Freeh, Director
Federal Bureau of Investigation
on
President's Fiscal Year 2000 Budget
Before the
Senate Committee on Appropriations
Subcommittee for the Departments of Commerce, Justice, and
State, the Judiciary, and Related Agencies
Washington, D.C.*

The Bombings in East Africa

On August 7, 1998, at approximately 10:40 a.m., local time, a bomb exploded near the United States Embassy in Dar es Salaam, Tanzania. Almost simultaneously, a bomb detonated near the United States Embassy in Nairobi, Kenya. The toll in both bombings, in terms of lives lost, persons injured, and damage to buildings, was substantial. In Dar es Salaam, 11 persons were killed, 7 of whom were foreign service nationals employed by the United States at the Embassy. Another 74 persons were injured, including 2 American citizens and 5 foreign service nationals. In Nairobi, where the United States Embassy was located in a congested downtown area, 213 persons were killed, including 12 American citizens and 32 foreign service nationals employed at the Embassy. Approximately 4,500 persons were treated for injuries, including 13 Americans and 16 foreign service nationals.

From the two crime scenes in Tanzania and Kenya, as well as from investigation and searches conducted in surrounding African nations and Pakistan, we collected and transported back to the FBI Laboratory more than three tons of evidentiary materials for examination and analysis. Our on-scene deployments in Dar es Salaam and Nairobi temporarily created what would have been among the largest FBI field offices in the United States.

As you can imagine, providing extended operational and administrative support to such a large overseas contingent was especially challenging and trying. It was not something that we accomplished on our own. In a large-scale overseas deployment such as East Africa, we must depend upon support and cooperation from our partners in the Departments of Defense and State. I would like to acknowledge the tremendous job performed by the men and women of the Departments of Defense and State under very adverse and trying circumstances. And, I am equally proud of the way our own personnel rose to meet the challenges presented by this difficult investigation.

We received exceptional cooperation and assistance from the governments of Tanzania and Kenya in conducting our investigation. They allowed us to recover and remove evidence for examination and transport it back to the United States. They also allowed us to conduct interviews and searches. The relationship established by our Legal Attache from Pretoria with Kenyan authorities was instrumental in that country's decision to allow the removal of two suspects for prosecution in the United States. We were also able to conduct investigation and searches in several other countries and locations.

As a result of these investigative efforts, 11 individuals associated with al-Qaeda, including Usama bin Laden, have each been indicted for conspiracy to kill United States nationals, the bombings of the United States Embassies in Tanzania and Kenya, and murder. One other individual, also an al-Qaeda member, has been indicted for conspiracy to kill United States nationals, perjury before a Federal Grand Jury, and lying to a Special Agent of the FBI. The progress and results that have been obtained in this case are the result of cooperation among many agencies, including the FBI, the Criminal Division, the United States Attorneys' offices in New York City and Washington, D.C., the Central Intelligence Agency, the Department of State, and Department of Defense, working together unselfishly in response to brutal acts of terrorism committed against the United States. Unfortunately, the bombing of United States Embassies in East Africa is only the latest in a series of international terrorist incidents directed against United States interests and policies.

The International Terrorist Situation

The current international terrorist threat can be divided into three general categories that represent a serious and distinct threat to the United States. These categories also reflect, to a large degree, how terrorists have adapted their tactics since the 1970's by learning from past successes and failures, from becoming familiar with law enforcement capabilities and tactics, and from exploiting technologies and weapons that are increasingly available to them in the post-Cold War era.

The first threat category, state sponsors of terrorism, violates every convention of international law. State sponsors of terrorism currently designated by the Department of State are: Iran, Iraq, Syria, Sudan, Libya, Cuba, and North Korea. Put simply, these nations view terrorism as a tool of foreign policy. In recent years, the terrorist activities of Cuba and North Korea appear to have declined as the economies of these countries have deteriorated. However, the terrorist activities of the other states I mentioned continue, and in some cases, have intensified during the past several years.

The second category of the international terrorist threat is represented by more formal terrorist organizations. These autonomous, generally transnational, organizations have their own infrastructures, personnel, financial arrangements, and training facilities. These organizations are able to plan and mount terrorist campaigns on an international basis and actively support terrorist activities in the United States.

The third category of international terrorist threat stems from loosely affiliated extremists, characterized by rogue terrorists such as Ramzi Ahmed Yousef and international terrorist financier Usama bin Laden. These loosely affiliated extremists may pose the most urgent threat to the United States because these individuals bring together groups on an ad hoc, temporary basis. By not being encumbered with the demands associated with maintaining a rigid, organizational infrastructure, these individuals are more difficult for law enforcement to track and infiltrate. Individuals such as Ramzi Yousef and Usama bin Laden have also demonstrated an ability to exploit mobility and technology to avoid detection and to conduct terrorist acts. Fortunately, in 1995, we were able to capture Yousef and return him to the United States to stand trial for the February 1993 bombing of the World Trade Center and the conspiracy to attack American aircraft overseas. Yousef was convicted in two trials and sentenced to life imprisonment.

* Source: http://www.fbi.gov/pressrm/congress/congress99/freehct2.htm

FBI TEN MOST WANTED FUGITIVE

MURDER OF U.S. NATIONALS OUTSIDE THE UNITED STATES; CONSPIRACY TO MURDER U.S. NATIONALS OUTSIDE THE UNITED STATES; ATTACK ON A FEDERAL FACILITY RESULTING IN DEATH

USAMA BIN LADEN

Date of Photograph Unknown

Aliases: Usama Bin Muhammad Bin Ladin, Shaykh Usama Bin Ladin, the Prince, the Emir, Abu Abdallah, Mujahid Shaykh, Hajj, the Director

DESCRIPTION

Date of Birth:	1957	**Hair:**	Brown
Place of Birth:	Saudi Arabia	**Eyes:**	Brown
Height:	6' 4" to 6' 6"	**Complexion:**	Olive
Weight:	Approximately 160 pounds	**Sex:**	Male
Build:	Thin	**Nationality:**	Saudi Arabian
Occupation(s):	Unknown		
Remarks:	He is the leader of a terrorist organization known as Al-Qaeda "The Base." He walks with a cane.		

CAUTION

USAMA BIN LADEN IS WANTED IN CONNECTION WITH THE AUGUST 7, 1998, BOMBINGS OF THE UNITED STATES EMBASSIES IN DAR ES SALAAM, TANZANIA AND NAIROBI, KENYA. THESE ATTACKS KILLED OVER 200 PEOPLE.

CONSIDERED ARMED AND EXTREMELY DANGEROUS

IF YOU HAVE ANY INFORMATION CONCERNING THIS PERSON, PLEASE CONTACT YOUR LOCAL FBI OFFICE OR THE NEAREST U.S. EMBASSY OR CONSULATE.

REWARD

The United States Government is offering a reward of up to $5 million for information leading directly to the apprehension or conviction of Usama Bin Laden.

www.fbi.gov

May 1999

WANTED

WANATAKIWA NA FBI | **BY THE** | مطلوب للإدالة
FBI | الـ يـ ا ـ الفد الي
(FBI) | ـ مـ ا ـ ـ سماـ ا ـ يه

FOR THE AUGUST 7, 1998 BOMBINGS OF THE U.S. EMBASSIES IN NAIROBI, KENYA AND DAR ES SALAAM, TANZANIA

KWA KULIPUA UBALOZI WA AMERIKANI MJINI NAIROBI, KENYA, NA MJINI DAR ES SALAAM, TANZANIA AGOSTI 7, 1998

ل يـا ـ د ـ في السـايـ ا ـ صـدييي في نـيـ ي يـا ا السلام اذ انيا في اغسطس .

SHEIKH AHMED SALIM SWEDAN
شيخ احمد سـالم سويدان

FAZUL ABDULLAH MOHAMED
فاضل عبد الله محمد

MUSTAFA MOHAMED FADHIL
مصطـ ي محمد فضل

FAHID MOHAMMED ALLY MSALAM
فهد محمد علي مسلم

KHALFAN KHAMIS MOHAMMED
خا ان خميس محمد

AHMED KHALFAN GHAILANI
احمد خا ان غيلاني

CAUTION - SHOULD BE CONSIDERED ARMED AND DANGEROUS
TAHADHARI - WATU HAWA WANA SILAHA NA NI HATARI
ـ يـ ـ خـ ـ يـ بـ ا ـ أشـا يـ بـ مسلحـ يـ : حـ د ي ـ

SERIKALI YA AMERIKANI INATOA ZAWADI KWA YEYOTE ATAKAYE TOA HABARI ZITAKAZO SABABISHA KUKAMATWA AU KUSHTAKIWA KWA HAWA WATU. WATU WATAKAO TOA HABARI HIZI WATAWEZA KUPEWA ZAWADI YA KUFIKIA $5 MILIONI (DOLA ZA AMERIKANI), KUHIFADHIWA KWA SIRI VITAMBULISHO VYA WATU HAO NA UWEZEKANO WA KUHAMISHWA WATU HAO PAMOJA NA JAMII ZAO.

Wasiliana na wachunguzi wa FBI moja kwa moja:

1) *KIBINAFSI -- Wasiliana na afisi za ubalozi au za wawakilishi wa Amerikani zilizo karibu*
2) *KWA BARUA -- FBI, Squad I-45 26 Federal Plaza New York, NY 10278 USA*
3) *KWA SIMU -- 1 - 212 - 964 - 0198*
4) *KWA FAX -- 1 - 212 - 384 - 8208*
5) *KWA E-MAIL -- africabomb@fbi.gov*

THE UNITED STATES GOVERNMENT IS OFFERING A REWARD FOR INFORMATION LEADING TO THE ARREST OR PROSECUTION OF THESE INDIVIDUALS. PERSONS PROVIDING INFORMATION ARE ELIGIBLE FOR A REWARD OF UP TO $5 MILLION U.S. DOLLARS, PROTECTION OF THEIR IDENTITY AND POSSIBLE RELOCATION FOR THEMSELVES AND THEIR FAMILY.

Contact FBI investigators directly:

1) IN PERSON -- Contact the nearest local U.S. Embassy or Consulate
2) BY MAIL -- FBI, Squad I-45 26 Federal Plaza New York, NY 10278 USA
3) BY PHONE -- 1 - 212 - 964 - 0198
4) BY FAX -- 1 - 212 - 384 - 8208
5) BY E-MAIL -- africabomb@fbi.gov

وم الـولـا يـ المحـ د امـ يـ يـ
مـ اف حـ د مليون ا ـ الـ ا ـ ي
يـ يـ د ـ يـ دـلـوما د ـ الـ ا ـ ي
عـلـ ا محاـ ـ ـ ا اشـا ـ . ل
ـ يدلي ـ لـوما يم الحماـ يم لهويـ ه
امـ نيـ يلـه و عـاذـ ه الـ
مـ ان ديد .

عـ ا ـ لـوما يـ ـ صـا ـ مـ
الـ يـ ا ـ الفد الى مباشـ :

FBI, Squad I-45
26 Federal Plaza
New York, NY 10278 USA

1-212-964-0198
1-212-384-8208
africabomb@fbi.gov

**Statement of the Director of Central Intelligence George J. Tenet
As Prepared for Delivery
Before the Senate Armed Services Committee Hearing on
Current and Projected National Security Threats***

2 February 1999

The Threat of Terrorism

On terrorism, Mr. Chairman, I must be frank in saying that Americans increasingly are the favored targets. US citizens and facilities suffered more than 35 percent of the total number of international terrorist attacks in 1998. This is up from 30 percent in 1997, and 25 percent in 1996.

Looking out over the next year, Mr. Chairman, let me mention two specific concerns. First, there is not the slightest doubt that Usama Bin Ladin, his worldwide allies, and his sympathizers are planning further attacks against us. Despite progress against his networks, Bin Ladin's organization has contacts virtually worldwide, including in the United States — and he has stated unequivocally, Mr. Chairman, that all Americans are targets.

Bin Ladin's overarching aim is to get the United States out of the Persian Gulf, but he will strike wherever in the world he thinks we are vulnerable. We are anticipating bombing attempts with conventional explosives, but his operatives are also capable of kidnappings and assassinations.

We have noted recent activity similar to what occurred prior to the African embassy bombings, Mr. Chairman, and I must tell you we are concerned that one or more of Bin Ladin's attacks could occur at any time.

One of my greatest concerns is the serious prospect that Bin Ladin or another terrorist might use chemical or biological weapons. Bin Ladin's organization is just one of about a dozen terrorist groups that have expressed an interest in or have sought chemical, biological, radiological, and nuclear (CBRN) agents. Bin Ladin, for example, has called the acquisition of these weapons a "religious duty" and noted that "how we use them is up to us." Earlier I referred to state sponsorship of terrorism, so let me take this opportunity to say, with respect to Iran, that we have yet to see any significant reduction in Iran's support for terrorism. President Khatami took office in August 1997, but hard-liners, such as Supreme leader Khamenei, continue to view terrorism as a legitimate tool of Iranian policy and they still control the institutions that can implement it.

* Source: http://www.cia.gov/cia/public_affairs/speeches/archives/1999/ps020299.html

J. Stapleton Roy
Assistant Secretary for Intelligence and Research
Statement Before the Senate Select Committee on Intelligence
Washington, DC, February 2, 2000*

Terrorism. The United States remains the number-one target of international terrorism. As in previous years, close to one-third of all incidents worldwide in the first 9 months of 1999 -- about 90 -- were directed against Americans. About 60 of these took place in Latin America and Western Europe, including the murder of three NGO workers in Colombia.

Increasingly, where attacks occur does not fully reflect the origin of the threat. The far-flung reach of Usama bin Ladin (UBL) from his base in Afghanistan is reflected in a continuous flurry of threats by his organization on almost every continent. Although we cannot attribute any of last year's anti-U.S. attacks to him, his transnational network and the devastating example of his 1998 attacks on the U.S. embassies in Kenya and Tanzania make him the primary threat to U.S. interests at home and abroad. Members of his network and other like-minded radical Islamic Mujahedin are active globally. Bin Ladin funds training camps and participates in a worldwide terrorist network. But he is not responsible for every Mujahedin attack. The UBL network is analogous to a large corporation with UBL as a CEO who provides guidance, funding, and logistical support. His supporters, like regional directors or affiliates, are not micromanaged, and may be left to follow separate agendas.

A number of terrorists including bin Ladin have evinced interest in acquiring weapons of mass destruction. So far, Aum Shinriyko, the group responsible for the 1995 subway gas attack in Tokyo, is the only group to use such a weapon on a large scale.

* Source: http://www.state.gov/www/policy_remarks/2000/000202_roy_security.html

Ambassador Michael Sheehan, Coordinator for Counter terrorism
Office of the Coordinator for Counter terrorism
Testimony Before the House International Relations Committee
Washington, DC, July 12, 2000*

Financing terrorism

When discussing the various causes of increased terrorist activity in South Asia, we must address the ability of terrorists to raise funds to support their activities. One of the most important ways to combat terrorism is to disrupt the financing of terrorist groups and activities. We have already made this a priority and are working hard--with unilateral and multilateral sanctions, bilateral diplomacy, and through the UN and G-8--to disrupt the financing of terrorism in South Asia. One notable success was the adoption by the UN General Assembly in December 1999 of the G-8 initiated International Convention for the Suppression of the Financing of Terrorism. Full implementation of this important new counter terrorism treaty by the largest number of governments is essential, and we hope to submit it to the Senate for advice and consent to ratification shortly.

But we must keep up the pressure. The ability of terrorists operating in Afghanistan, for example, to obtain funds and other material support is a symptom of the other primary trend in terrorism that I described in Patterns: the shift from terrorist groups sponsored by states to international networks of terrorists not affiliated with particular governments.

This shift has profound implications for our policies in South Asia. The capabilities of Usama Bin Ladin's al-Qa'ida network, which has centered itself within Afghanistan, demonstrate why this is the case. Bin Ladin's organization operates on its own, without having to depend on a state sponsor for material support. He has financial resources and means of raising funds, often through narco-trafficking or the use of legitimate "front" companies. He enjoys international financial support. Bin Ladin and other non-state terrorists also benefit from the globalization of communication, using e-mail and Internet websites to spread their message, recruit new members, and raise funds.

These capabilities allow Bin Ladin and other terrorists to extend their tentacles around the world. Terrorist networks outside the context of the international state system provide everything that is needed for groups such as the Egyptian Islamic Jihad (EIJ) to survive and become stronger - even when they are based in friendly states with vigorous counter terrorism policies. The threat posed by this group, a faction of which is closely allied to Bin Ladin, illustrates the challenges we face as non-state terrorism becomes more prevalent.

The role of the Taliban

The ability of groups such as al-Qa'ida to plan and carry out terrorist attacks with impunity brings us to the final causal factor in the shift of terrorism to South Asia: the Taliban's refusal to crack down on terrorists. Afghanistan has become the primary swamp of terrorism, harboring terrorists from the region and around the world. The Taliban, which controls most Afghan territory, provides safe haven for Usama Bin Ladin and his network. Because of the room, which the Taliban gives him to operate, Bin Ladin has created a truly transnational terrorist enterprise, drawing on recruits from across Asia, Africa, and Europe, as well as the Middle East. The Taliban has also given logistic support to members of other terrorist organizations, such as the Egyptian Islamic Jihad, the Algerian Armed Islamic group, Kashmiri separatists, and a number of militant organizations from Central Asia, including terrorists from Uzbekistan and Tajikistan.

United Nations Resolutions

United
Nations

S/RES/1267 (1999)
15 October 1999

RESOLUTION 1267 (1999)

Adopted by the Security Council at its 4051st meeting, on 15 October 1999 *

The Security Council,

Reaffirming its previous resolutions, in particular resolutions 1189 (1998) of 13 August 1998, 1193 (1998) of 28 August 1998 and 1214 (1998) of 8 December 1998, and the statements of its President on the situation in Afghanistan,

Reaffirming its strong commitment to the sovereignty, independence, territorial integrity and national unity of Afghanistan, and its respect for Afghanistan's cultural and historical heritage,

Reiterating its deep concern over the continuing violations of international humanitarian law and of human rights, particularly discrimination against women and girls, and over the significant rise in the illicit production of opium, and stressing that the capture by the Taliban of the Consulate-General of the Islamic Republic of Iran and the murder of Iranian diplomats and a journalist in Mazar-e-Sharif constituted flagrant violations of established international law,

Recalling the relevant international counter-terrorism conventions and in particular the obligations of parties to those conventions to extradite or prosecute terrorists,

Strongly condemning the continuing use of Afghan territory, especially areas controlled by the Taliban, for the sheltering and training of terrorists and planning of terrorist acts, and reaffirming its conviction that the suppression of international terrorism is essential for the maintenance of international peace and security,

Deploring the fact that the Taliban continues to provide safe haven to Usama bin Laden and to allow him and others associated with him to operate a network of terrorist training camps from Taliban-controlled territory and to use Afghanistan as a base from which to sponsor international terrorist operations,

Noting the indictment of Usama bin Laden and his associates by the United States of America for, inter alia, the 7 August 1998 bombings of the United States embassies in Nairobi, Kenya, and Dar es Salaam, Tanzania and for conspiring to kill American nationals outside the United States, and noting also the request of the United States of America to the Taliban to surrender them for trial (S/1999/1021),

Determining that the failure of the Taliban authorities to respond to the demands in paragraph 13 of resolution 1214 (1998) constitutes a threat to international peace and security,

Stressing its determination to ensure respect for its resolutions,

Acting under Chapter VII of the Charter of the United Nations,

1. Insists that the Afghan faction known as the Taliban, which also calls itself the Islamic Emirate of Afghanistan, comply promptly with its previous resolutions and in particular

cease the provision of sanctuary and training for international terrorists and their organizations, take appropriate effective measures to ensure that the territory under its control is not used for terrorist installations and camps, or for the preparation or organization of terrorist acts against other States or their citizens, and cooperate with efforts to bring indicted terrorists to justice;

2. Demands that the Taliban turn over Usama bin Laden without further delay to appropriate authorities in a country where he has been indicted, or to appropriate authorities in a country where he will be returned to such a country, or to appropriate authorities in a country where he will be arrested and effectively brought to justice;

3. Decides that on 14 November 1999 all States shall impose the measures set out in paragraph 4 below, unless the Council has previously decided, on the basis of a report of the Secretary-General, that the Taliban has fully complied with the obligation set out in paragraph 2 above;

4. Decides further that, in order to enforce paragraph 2 above, all States shall:

(a) Deny permission for any aircraft to take off from or land in their territory if it is owned, leased or operated by or on behalf of the Taliban as designated by the Committee established by paragraph 6 below, unless the particular flight has been approved in advance by the Committee on the grounds of humanitarian need, including religious obligation such as the performance of the Hajj;

(b) Freeze funds and other financial resources, including funds derived or generated from property owned or controlled directly or indirectly by the Taliban, or by any undertaking owned or controlled by the Taliban, as designated by the Committee established by paragraph 6 below, and ensure that neither they nor any other funds or financial resources so designated are made available, by their nationals or by any persons within their territory, to or for the benefit of the Taliban or any undertaking owned or controlled, directly or indirectly, by the Taliban, except as may be authorized by the Committee on a case-by-case basis on the grounds of humanitarian need;

5. Urges all States to cooperate with efforts to fulfil the demand in paragraph 2 above, and to consider further measures against Usama bin Laden and his associates;

6. Decides to establish, in accordance with rule 28 of its provisional rules of procedure, a Committee of the Security Council consisting of all the members of the Council to undertake the following tasks and to report on its work to the Council with its observations and recommendations:

(a) To seek from all States further information regarding the action taken by them with a view to effectively implementing the measures imposed by paragraph 4 above;

(b) To consider information brought to its attention by States concerning violations of the measures imposed by paragraph 4 above and to recommend appropriate measures in response thereto;

(c) To make periodic reports to the Council on the impact, including the humanitarian implications, of the measures imposed by paragraph 4 above;

(d) To make periodic reports to the Council on information submitted to it regarding alleged violations of the measures imposed by paragraph 4 above, identifying where possible persons or entities reported to be engaged in such violations;

(e) To designate the aircraft and funds or other financial resources referred to in paragraph 4 above in order to facilitate the implementation of the measures imposed by that paragraph;

(f) To consider requests for exemptions from the measures imposed by paragraph 4 above as provided in that paragraph, and to decide on the granting of an exemption to these measures in respect of the payment by the International Air Transport Association (IATA) to the aeronautical authority of Afghanistan on behalf of international airlines for air traffic control services;

(g) To examine the reports submitted pursuant to paragraph 9 below;

7. Calls upon all States to act strictly in accordance with the provisions of this resolution, notwithstanding the existence of any rights or obligations conferred or imposed by any

international agreement or any contract entered into or any licence or permit granted prior to the date of coming into force of the measures imposed by paragraph 4 above;

8. Calls upon States to bring proceedings against persons and entities within their jurisdiction that violate the measures imposed by paragraph 4 above and to impose appropriate penalties;

9. Calls upon all States to cooperate fully with the Committee established by paragraph 6 above in the fulfilment of its tasks, including supplying such information as may be required by the Committee in pursuance of this resolution;

10. Requests all States to report to the Committee established by paragraph 6 above within 30 days of the coming into force of the measures imposed by paragraph 4 above on the steps they have taken with a view to effectively implementing paragraph 4 above;

11. Requests the Secretary-General to provide all necessary assistance to the Committee established by paragraph 6 above and to make the necessary arrangements in the Secretariat for this purpose;

12. Requests the Committee established by paragraph 6 above to determine appropriate arrangements, on the basis of recommendations of the Secretariat, with competent international organizations, neighbouring and other States, and parties concerned with a view to improving the monitoring of the implementation of the measures imposed by paragraph 4 above;

13. Requests the Secretariat to submit for consideration by the Committee established by paragraph 6 above information received from Governments and public sources on possible violations of the measures imposed by paragraph 4 above;

14. Decides to terminate the measures imposed by paragraph 4 above once the Secretary-General reports to the Security Council that the Taliban has fulfilled the obligation set out in paragraph 2 above;

15. Expresses its readiness to consider the imposition of further measures, in accordance with its responsibility under the Charter of the United Nations, with the aim of achieving the full implementation of this resolution;

16. Decides to remain actively seized of the matter.

* Source: http://www.un.org/Docs/scres/1999/99sc1267.htm

United Nations Security Council Resolution 1333 (2000)
December 19, 2000

on the Situation in Afghanistan

PDF file

http://www.un.org/Docs/scres/2000/res1333e.pdf